Sunny Side Up
The Gritty Memoirs of a Crazy Chica

Holly Kay Cronk

ISBN 978-0-692-57261-0

DEDICATION

To my husband Scott and our three children
Zac, Jake and Katy. You are the loves of my life.
Always remember the bad days never last forever
I will always love you more-
Mom

To my big brother Brad and little sister Mandy,
You guys bring something very special to my life.
Thank you for everything. Here's to making happy memories!
I Love you

ONE

Shutting the front door behind me, I shuffle through the snow covered walkway to my shop. It's the day after Christmas, a Christmas that was the toughest one I have ever had. It had been nothing more than any other day... another unremarkable day. One of over 365 days before it that I had struggled through trying so very hard to not let my friends and family know how much my heart was broken. How much I hurt and how desperate I was for answers. I didn't want to shut the door. I didn't want to say goodbye to my husband. I didn't want to leave my sanctuary on the Ferluknat Farm because I didn't know if I would be the same when I returned. What if when I came home I was a bigger mess? That was a possible outcome and I knew it.

 I had no hope left. The only way I had managed to function was to keep moving forward and pray. On the outside I was HollyKay, on the inside there was nothing but a drowning pool of tears. As the garage door rolls up and I back my car out of the shop I bit my lip holding back 47 years of emotions. Doubting I had the strength left to handle what lie before me I eased my 2011 Ford Taurus out on the road and headed to the interstate and ultimately to my destination.

As the miles passed, the apprehension slowly gave way to other thoughts and memories. I adjusted my car seat and settled in for a long days ride. I'm committed now. There are people waiting to see me, they seem to be excited to see me. I had tried to get out of coming on this trip as my son totaled his Jeep a few days before Christmas and I just knew he would need me to stick around. Never one for pathetic excuses, my first attempt was a fail, as he was just a little bruised up and would be ok with his father at the farm.

All of these feelings of the last months were not like me. I wasn't like me anymore. Hell, I didn't know who I was anymore. I was just living, breathing and hoping no one caught on to the zombie that walked among them. I couldn't imagine anyone being excited to see me I was a fucking mess in disguise.

Setting the cruise control, I plug my phone into the charger and then decide to scan the radio for some good road tunes. First rattle out of the box I happen upon an oldies country channel. Since this whole ordeal blew up I haven't listened to country music like this as it reminded me too much of people and times that were once in my life. I couldn't bear it before. *"Hey, if you happen to see the most beautiful girl in the world would you tell her I love her? Would you tell her I need her so."* I always loved Charlie Rich. The center stripes on the highway race by like the sprockets on a movie reel and the blacktop becomes a movie screen as my mind starts to play a montage of events and unrelated memories play out. Little snippets of my life, parts of trips made through the last 30 years on the very same roads I will travel on this day. This old stretch of highway and I go way back. My God where have the years gone and why do they seem like they were for nothing now? I miss my 29" waist and perky boobs. What happened to that carefree girl? Thankfully, as the songs changed so to do the memories. Charlie Rich gives way to Charlie Pride. All he wants to do is kiss a beautiful girl in the morning and all I want to do is wake up from this nightmare. *"As the snow flies on a cold and gray Chicago morning A poor little baby child is born In the ghetto And his mama cries ."* Elvis Presley and his deep soft voice take over the airwaves and for the first time I really felt this song and then I felt ashamed that I was being such a "ball licker" about my life and what it has come to. Welcome to the roller coaster, merry-go round that spins out of control in my mind and rules my existence. Apparently my ticket to ride is for a nonstop; proceed at mach 5 speed ride. I can't take it any longer, as the tears begin to soak the collar of my sweater I use the cuff of my sleeve to wipe away the trails they leave on my cheeks. I can't stop them, this isn't the first time.

From my farm to work it's 10 miles of beautiful countryside. This equates into 15 minutes of solo time twice a day. And usually ends up with me sobbing. Ten years ago when my life was in the shitter, the last time, I realized that I had to allow myself to cry. For the most part I viewed it as a sign of weakness. I could tell by my hard-ass views on life and my hardball way of doing business that this practice had also made me cold hearted when it came to sensitivity and compassion for others. I didn't just wake up one morning a fully-fledged hard ass bitch. No, no, no my training began the day I was born. This novel idea of allowing myself to cry didn't come easily. And "getting in touch with my feelings" seemed as foreign to me as sitting in a circle of strangers and singing Kumbaya. I might as well run naked through a shopping mall. I couldn't expose myself and vulnerabilities any more than that, so crying was hard to do at the beginning. I knew in my heart most of this road trip was going to end up with me crying and so I did.

The minutes and the miles rolled on by and I cried over everything. I cried over the lost innocence of a childhood. I cried over a lost identity. I cried over my failures as a parent. I cried over missing the times that passed that were good. I cried over thoughts and fears I have that my dreams may never come to fruition. I cried because I work so hard to be better, do better, and move up in this world yet my life has been nothing but one shit storm after another. Despite that I kept smiling, stayed positive and focused... until now. I cried because it scares the hell out of me that the second half of my life will be exactly like the first half was. I cried because even though I know God is always with me I really wished He would cut me some slack. I cried because that's all I had left inside me, after all, something had to fill the void.

It was dark the morning I left for Colorado. Thank God for that. No one that I passed on the roads could see how awful I looked. Soon a blush of pink slowly crept up on the eastern horizon behind me. I could see it in my rearview mirror. The coffee in my travel mug had given out a couple hours before. I needed some rejuvenation. Driving with one hand and using the other to rifle through my console for some clean dry napkins to wipe my face with, I steadily approach an exit to a truck stop. My face wasn't too puffy; I could pass for just being road wore. Maybe with a sunny smile nobody would catch on that I really just spent the last hours feeling sorry for myself.

Traveling nowadays is much different than when I was a kid. It just seems there are more weirdos out there now. I pull into the truck stop and park where I can easily get to and from my vehicle and can be seen doing it. I had made the last minute decision to leave my usual traveling buddy, Chief, at home. Chief is a .38 special revolver given to me when I was about 20 years old by someone I loved very much. It has served silently and faithfully all this time, first protecting just me, and then my family as I had kids. When I'm not on a road trip it rests always ready by my bed should it be called to service. I wished I had brought it this time as I really couldn't feel more vulnerable right now. I don't really know why I chose not to bring it. Maybe it's because I didn't really care if anything happened to me on this trip. Maybe it was because the memories attached to it are still so very painful and I just don't want to hurt anymore. I step out of my car and make sure to lock it and walk into the store.

Going pee and getting coffee are my main objectives. Fulfilling the first task, I move on to obtaining some creamer with a little coffee - another sign of how the years have taken their toll. In earlier times nothing was worth drinking if I couldn't drink it straight. That included whiskey and coffee, despite being told by my doctor I can't drink coffee. I still do as a matter of fact - it is my only vice nowadays, as alcohol and a few other things I did when I was younger are definitely no-nos. Besides, I figure with enough creamer it really can't technically be called coffee. It's just a coffee flavored drink.

My husband drives truck and hauls steel for a huge corporation and so I know all too well the life of a trucker. It must have been a surprise to the fellow that befriended me as we waited in line to checkout when he struck up a conversation. The gist of it was he had been stuck there over Christmas. Home was in Maine and he would be lucky to make it there by New Years.

I quipped, "You must be at the mercy of a dispatcher."

He smiled and agreed. I paid for my coffee and turned around, wishing him a Merry Christmas and telling him as I walked out the door to drive safe and that I hoped he would make it home soon.

Still aware of my surroundings as I walked back to my car, I said a little prayer for that guy. (Whoever you are I really do hope you made it home.) I didn't expect much when I walked in, but as I was walking out my spirits were lifted by the smiling Merry Christmas wishing cashier and the conversation I had with the trucker from Maine. Both total strangers who just by their smiles and cordialness changed the course of my day. If their smiles did that for me I wondered if I ever had that same impact on others with mine. I Hoped so. You can call it searching, call it what you want, but I thanked God for that respite from my self-pity party, I am sure He placed them there in my life and it worked.

TWO

Almost halfway to my destination I decided I would stop at the next rest area, go pee... of course, and put on some make-up. It had been a while since my crying fest and I figured it was safe to get prettied up. Funny, I looked better on the outside than I felt on the inside. By no means was I airbrushed pretty but if I could feel as good as I looked that would still have been a huge improvement. I looked like a rainbow but I was filled with black.

For the first time EVER I managed to score great radio stations and awesome tunes all the way across Nebraska and Colorado. Used to be all you could get was Hell Fire and Brimstone stations. If you didn't have cassettes or CD's you were either traveling in silence, or listening to some preacher you never heard of. Songs seem to play at the right time they either fit my mood or thoughts and it made the miles fly. I decided at the last minute I was going to come across Highway 14 through Sterling and across the Pawnee National Grasslands into Fort Collins and on to Douglass Lake. It was a very nostalgic route that I hadn't taken in years. Even though this was supposed to be a very covert operation I still took a picture of the Colorado state sign and texted it to my sister. I knew she was excited about this visit and I was even getting excited now by the little things that came together during my trip so far that lifted me up. Apprehension and nervousness were both still there in the back of my mind. The reassuring thought came as well; I can always get in my car and leave if it all goes to shit.

The Sterling exit came up and I slowed down, time spun backwards as I drove passed the places I remembered from my childhood. It wasn't the same, who was I kidding? Progress had changed the face of the town and the lies and betrayal stole any fondness I had for it. Naturally, the last thing I saw leaving town was a huge Wal-Mart Supercenter. I guess you can never get away from the Evil Empire.

 I never liked that stretch of road on Hwy 14 between Sterling and Ault. As a kid it seemed to last forever and ever. There was never anything out there to occupy a kid's attention.   As I came around a curve near Stoneham I had to smile the one thing that seemed to never change was the one room school house building that stood on top of a hill next to the highway. It was like an ageless, timeless sentinel. It looked no different that day than it did all those years ago. Although weathered and abandoned it still was a testimony to sturdy workmanship. If it could talk it would have probably said I am over a 100 hundred years old, I have survived countless tornados and storms that have swept across these plains. My walls are sturdy and strong and at one time my windows had glass and I sheltered the children that came to me as they learned their reading and writing. Even though I have been abandoned all these years I am still standing.   A building that once served as a road marker now became something more.

It seemed all too quick when Briggsdale came into view and I could see some of the Rockies. Briggsdale holds a lot of memories for me; it too seemed so foreign now. As I looked at the Rockies, shocked there was no smog trailing up the foothills to hide it from view, in the same thought of how pretty they were I also realized I really hadn't missed them as much in the last year and a half as I used to. I knew why and the thought just crushed my heart. Briggsdale was once only an agricultural community, homesteaded years ago by farmers who grew wheat and raised cattle on it. Families knew each other and they survived together what time and nature brought their way. Now it's congested with crazy driving people, oil and gas rigs and transfer stations. The only landmark still standing was what I grew up calling Soppo's Bar. Even now it's got a different name, its owner of years ago long since passed away. It seems like man won't stop at anything to drill and pump every drop of blood from our beautiful planet; that's not progress, that's greed.

The light was green in Ault so I never even slowed down as I passed through. The buildings never gave out all the way to Fort Collins. Housing developments had filled most of the stretch of miles between the two towns. I turned the GPS on my phone and waited for directions to Douglass Lake.

Some of the area was familiar to me but the closer to the foothills I got the more I wondered if my GPS knew where I needed to go. After some turns and curves and dirt roads I turned to drive down a long driveway leading to the house and small farm my sister was taking care of. Its owners were "Snow Birds", they stay in Arizona during the winter and spend their spring and summers in Colorado. As I pulled up to the house there she was, my kid sister Mandy.

THREE

Mandy is eight years younger than I. In addition to the age difference, circumstances in our childhoods and lives kept us from ever being very close, at least not like I would have liked. As we have grown older we have become much closer and I adore her. Her life in the past year hasn't been any better than mine and I couldn't be more grateful for her.

We hug and exchange small chat as I shake off the stiffness of driving all day. My brother had already called several times to see if I was there yet and was on his way at that moment to meet us. So to kill time and my nerves I went with her to do some chores and take care of the dogs and cats, see the horse and mule and get a grand tour of the farm.

The gathering that was to take place was a monumental one, an event that had never happened before. Our mother had made sure to keep us pitted against each other by throwing us each under the bus to the other. She would bad mouth my sister to me and vice versa. When our brother had anything to do with her she did the same thing.   Brad cut her out of his life 19 years ago, about 2 years after that he quit having anything to do with me.

I was about to see my big brother in person. For the last 16 years I had only seen pictures that Mandy sent me. Up until a few months ago I hadn't even heard from Brad. Then he started to email me and we started to get to know each other again. I never knew why he stopped talking to me. I spent years speculating and then just being mad and hurt and then I just gave up. Whatever the reason, it must have been a good one and I was going to respect his decision. It was all I could do and it kind of helped me deal with it better.

None of that mattered now. I was so nervous to see him after all these years. I just wanted to run away from it all. Would he like me? Would I make him mad again and have this all end up terribly? Would he just get up and leave and that would be it? Would he be short with me and tell me I'm awful? Dear God, I just wanted to not disappoint him. He was my big brother and we did grow up together, kind of; I still looked up to him and even at my age I found it silly but undeniable that I needed his approval and acceptance.

Soon enough a red suburban with a cloud of dust behind it turned into the driveway and headed towards us.

Mandy said, '' That's Brad, Hol.''

Hol is short for Holly and only my sister, brother and mother have called me that. I was trembling inside and frozen on the outside as the suburban drove up to us and stopped. The man I remembered years ago was now white haired he looked like Buffalo Bill Cody with a little Wilford Brimley thrown in. He looked beautiful and wonderful and then I heard his voice.

"It's been a long time! You look good Holly!"

"Ohh" I reply, "I'm just fat and out of shape."

Getting out of his truck he reaches out and hugs me I hear him whisper again in my ear, "It's been a long time Holly."

Stand back boys it's a gusher! The sound of his voice and to feel his arms around me again made me sob. I tried to stop and stand on my own.

He said, "It's alright girl it's alright."

And we held each other and cried. When I could finally stop we looked at each other, all I wanted to do was look into his face and see his eyes and that smile.

The three of us spent the night drinking a little and talking a lot. I took a chance on drinking some good German Riesling wine and didn't make it very far before I'd had enough but it was the conversation that meant the most to me. I hung on every minute and every word, thoroughly enjoying gabbing and regaling the past with my sister and brother. Our kids had all grown up and gone out into the world. Brad had divorced a long time ago, my sister just recently. Through the years I never lost touch with my sister. We have always had a relationship on some level and she had always maintained a relationship with Brad as well. It may have been my idea originally to drive out but it was Mandy that made the reunion possible.

FOUR

I grew up believing that Brad and I were full siblings and Mandy was our half sibling. Brad and I adored our dad. He was our world, our rock and we looked up to him. Our mother was lenient in allowing us to be with our father after they split. We spent weekends and vacations and many holidays with him and his family, the Hilzer's. Our parents had divorced when I was very little and so I never grew up knowing what it was like to have both my parents together. When she allowed us that time with our father we paid a heavy price.

My brother and I would wait anxiously for our father to arrive to pick us up on those occasions. No matter what our dad drove, Cadillac, El Camino, whatever we knew the sound of the engine. As we would anxiously wait for him to arrive we would try to watch TV to pass the time but our ears were always perked for that engine sound. Sometimes we would race to the window on a false alarm, mostly me as my brother was better at it. Our bags would be packed and by the door. The minute he would pull up we were gone like a flash down the sidewalk and in his vehicle. I always sat in the middle. I had the best spot right next to my daddy. I felt like a princess and that was my throne.

Often we would stop at a place called Johnsons Corner on I-25 by Loveland Colorado or a restaurant called the Dolls House on Colfax in Denver. Our dad would have coffee and my brother and I would have shakes. Strawberry was my favorite.

It was such a contradiction for our mother to allow us so much time with our dad, let us talk to him on the phone and pack our bags for us. It didn't make any sense to us to face her hateful tone and cutting words upon our return. There wasn't a visit that went by that both of us did not dread returning home. Bert would wait till the last possible moment we had to leave. Often I was in tears because I didn't want to go home. My brother always tried to be strong but it got him too. There were times we just held each other; we knew what we faced going home. It never failed; there was no way to avoid a verbal assault by her. Even if we tried to avoid her by going straight to our rooms she would still start something. Generally it was with my brother first. Our Mother's sarcastic tone and words degraded and belittled our father and demeaned the time we spent with him. She used words like "Big Man, shooting guns... bang bang." She was referring to the fact that our father was a gunsmith. Brad and I loved to go shooting with our dad and she knew it. She would try to tear him and us down. Brad would stand up to her and so would I when I got old enough to be involved in her rants. We tried desperately to defend our father and ourselves, never knowing why or what it was that made her behave this way but still deeply affected by her wrath. She would call us belligerent and motor mouths. Brad would end up going to his room and I would end up crying in mine. My confidant, Cindi the stuffed Bear, would cuddle me and I would cry so hard she'd be wet from the tears.

We knew we faced this when our dad would drop us off. We could always feel the tension when we would walk through the door but we never knew if it would be something we said or did that would make her flip. And it didn't matter how hard we tried to avoid it, it still happened more often than not.

It was always such a release and relief to be with our father and the Hilzer's. They accepted us unconditionally and loved us. We knew it, we felt it. Our mother's side of the family was completely opposite. I never felt at ease among them. Our grandfather Henry never approved of our father. He ignorantly called him a "Red" short for Russian. The relationship our mother had with her family was strained at best. And we could feel it. She tried to make it seem like something other than that. You can candy coat a turd, but it still stinks and so did this whole situation.

We always thought it was all them, that we were the black sheep all because of them. Now I think my mother and her sisters all have emotional issues and that possibly my mother is the worse among them. We never fit in, we both tried but our grandparents were for the most part superficial and narrow minded. What few good memories I had of them were erased once I realized this. It was by God's grace that we weren't exposed to them anymore than we were or we would be no better than them or our mother. It was a blessing and a saving grace that we somehow managed to always be with the Hilzer's and we were more influenced by their good nature and genuine love. It was a terrible thing that we paid such a price for those precious moments enduring our mother's erratic behavior.

FIVE

Brad is five years older than me and his memory goes back further than mine which was an immense help when we spoke of the past. Thankfully he remembers addresses and names. Brad has probably spent as much time as I had in the last years trying to understand our years growing up. In doing so he also acquired something I never even gave a second thought to, an unbiased view point of the Hilzer's and our father. His insight offered a new perspective.

My love for him was renewed that night. He was such a joy to listen to and talk to. As we sat around the dining room table I wished we were all more than half siblings. But the truth of it is we aren't. It was that discovery that lead to this reunion. Looking in his face searching for physical similarities, finding them and realizing they could only be from our mother and not our father just made my heart sink. Not only because I'm not a Hilzer but because I didn't know who I was anymore.

Growing up I was always told how much I resembled my grandma Hilzer. She was 4 ft something and round. She had the most marvelous pixie sparkle in her eyes and she could be ornery when she wanted to. Grandma was a great cook and knew how to make German food. She was an avid sewer and crocheted a lot. Every night she read her bible before bed and every Sunday she watched her favorite TV preacher. My memories of her are all good and I loved her so very much. As a little girl she was my role model I took after her in many ways. She would even sew me clothes, cute outfits that were similar to hers. There were even some physical similarities; we were both chubby for one.

My mother always made a big deal about my blood type AB RH-negative. The rarest blood type there is. I was led to believe I was a blessing and that my existence was nothing short of miraculous. It would be these very things that would be my mother's undoing.

As kids we would be subjected to hearing verbal exchanges of hate outside our rooms or even as we watched TV. Our mother would be on the phone arguing with our father. I don't know what our father was saying but we sure could hear our mother and the hate and hurtful things that came from her mouth were something kids don't need to hear. I'm not sure how I became aware of some barber named Pete that she was supposed to have had a fling with but I was aware of it and her adamant denial it ever took place.

Around late 2009 my mother found out she had bladder cancer and it needed to be removed. The surgery was extensive and would be a lengthy hospital stay. So I took family medical leave, packed my bags, left my husband and kids and went to Colorado to stay with her in the hospital. I did this out of love and compassion, I knew she was scared. Anyone would be. I didn't want her to be alone. I was gone for two weeks and lived in the hospital from the time she was admitted till I had to come home. I didn't want to leave her in the hospital but her recovery was taking longer than I could stay from my home and so I had to go. I slept when she slept and was awake when she was awake. I checked on her through the night. I helped with her care and did everything I could. It was difficult to see her like that but it was harder on her to be in that way. My bed was a hard padded hospital reclining chair next to her bed. I didn't get the impression that my presence was appreciated by the hospital staff, however, it was at her bidding that I was there and so I did my duty as her daughter.

Although my mother will deny this vehemently it is true that she never liked it when any of us kids would have conversations or do things without her being there. It's hard to describe. But I know it's part of her mental illness. We figured she was always overly concerned that we would talk about her and figure things out that would contradict what she would have us believe. Most times this paranoia would be unfounded. It's ironic that due to her mental illness, we had on occasion discussed questionable things past and present that she was involved in.

 During a break I took from her, Mandy and I were sitting in a visitor's area talking and while I have no recollection how it came up the topic of my parentage was discussed. I remember that I had no feelings either way about it. I wasn't shocked, I wasn't instantly heartbroken I was just numb. It was like I had already been through so much in my life up until then some of which was brought to bear by her and some of which came with my marriage and other childhood events. Honestly, what next? This is just the cherry I can plop on the pile of shit I have swept in the corner of my mind. It just didn't surprise me, it was like it made sense and I have no idea why.

Knowing that Bert might not be my biological father didn't make any difference in how I cared for my mother for the rest of my stay. I did the best I could and I left her knowing that.

SIX

Back and forth I wrestled with this tidbit of knowledge. Months would go by. I'd try to just let it go and keep moving on trying to be grateful for having the Hilzers in my life. I tried not focusing on how things could have been and if my life would be better if I knew for sure.

Years passed, wondering and trying to put memories and stories together. I had a cedar chest in my bedroom that contained over a hundred years of records and pictures chronicling the Hilzer family. I was convinced it held the answer to this secret. In a way it did. On occasion I would browse through it looking for anything that would be helpful. Hoping something would spark an idea or be a clue. I was looking at pictures reading dates and just grasping at anything that could prove or disprove the rumors and things I heard. The obvious thing would be to ask Brad to do a DNA test but he was estranged from the family, I didn't blame him and I wasn't going to interfere with it. I was hopeful he knew Bert's blood type and Mandy asked him but he couldn't remember. I researched paternity testing, DNA and blood types. Finally I made some headway. As it turns out my blood type, being so rare and all, worked in my favor. The only blood type from either parent that could not result in an AB RH -negative baby is 0. I knew my mother's was probably blood type A. If I could get proof of Bert's blood type it would be a step forward. As I went through the cedar chest the answer stared me in the face. Bert was in the Navy - maybe there was an avenue there. I doubted they had DNA collection at that time but they would have physical records. I researched on the internet and found that luckily his dates of enlistment fell within a time frame I could write for these records. So I downloaded, printed and filled out the form. I had to tell them why I needed the information so I checked for family medical history and paternity. I realized then I was fully committed to finding out the truth and that it did mean something to me. Within two weeks I got the information they had available and it was all I needed. Bert was 0 positive blood type; there was no way he was my father. My heart sank instantly. I didn't know what to do next but I knew nothing would be the same ever again for me.

Confirming my parentage, or lack thereof, hadn't thrown me in a tailspin just yet. I had thoughts that maybe my mother knew but wasn't going to say anything till she was on her deathbed. I still tried to reason with it. I tried to come up with some way to live with the knowledge but not do anything about it. I had told Mandy and my husband Scott about it but I don't know what I expected to accomplish by doing so. There was nothing they could say or do. What do you say to someone you love when they find out this kind of information? They were speechless for a while and then came the attempt to smooth things over by saying I was still Hilzer and Bert was my dad anyway. They were all very nice attempts but not the truth.

I always thought I looked a lot like my Uncle Paul. After all, he had been tossed up as a possible sperm donor towards my existence. I had heard rumors of an affair between him and my mother. That would make sense if it were true. But my Aunt Judy, his wife, was still alive at that time and she was my dad's sister. Even though Judy and Paul were alcoholics most of their lives I always liked them both. They were always happy and they were part of the only family that I really felt love from. I didn't want to cause any more hurt than what was already being felt. I wasn't trying to be a martyr I was just trying to do the right thing by everyone. What a mess this would cause and how many more people would be hurt that didn't need to be. My Aunt Judy and her three kids would be the top four people. I decided to focus on my own kids and let the matter go for a while, see if maybe since Mandy knew what was going on and she did tell Brad I knew maybe something would come up. So I waited again.

Months down the road, out of the blue I got a letter from my Aunt Joann. (My dad had two sisters, Joann and Judy. Their birth order was: Bert, Joann and then Judy.) The disbelief of what she wrote caused me to drop the letter on the kitchen counter and fall into my chair in shock and sadness. Aunt Judy had passed away three weeks earlier from colon cancer. She went quickly and it was a huge blow to her family. I couldn't figure out why Aunt Joann didn't call me when it happened but she was 80 years old I'm not going to second guess her. I was grateful she wrote me and so I called her and she told me how it all happened. I asked about Paul and the kids and how they were doing. I told her I felt terrible that I wasn't there for the funeral but that to keep my phone number handy in case she needed anything. The day I called was the day of a memorial they were having for my Aunt Judy and so we didn't talk long. Hanging up the phone the thought that I wasn't there for my possible siblings and father tore another piece of my heart. Something in the back of my mind just kept telling me this wasn't going to be some big surprise to him or my mother.

SEVEN

Mandy's marriage had run its course and so she and her husband Rusty split for good. They shared a son, so they still had to come together for his sake but the family was still split. My mother left her apartment in Cheyenne Wyoming and came to live with Mandy and her son. This was a terrible idea and I told them both that. I knew it wasn't going to work and it would be an absolute mess but Mandy needed the help and our mother needed to be closer to her doctors. You could put two feral male cats in a room together and have a better chance of them getting along than you would putting these two women under one roof. How lucky was I to be the recipient of my mother's texts throwing her own daughter under the bus and Mandy texting me about how catty our mother was... DUHHHHH told you soooo!!!

It wasn't long and the fur was flying. Matters would settle down for a while but always the constant texts from my mother about Mandy and her son. Months went by, they managed to make it almost a year under the same roof before it happened. In a fit of hurt and anger Mandy blurted to our mother that I knew Bert wasn't my father. Then the unexpected phone call came.

When I answered the call my mother's shrill and frantic sounding voice came across and it made my skin crawl. It made me want to jump out of my body and run away screaming for a release from the insanity I knew was on the other end of the line.

"Hi mom what's up?" I answered.

"Holly? Well I don't know apparently Manda just told me you know Bert isn't your father?"

"Well mom I'll tell you, no he isn't. "

"Ohhh that's impossible why do you look so much like your grandma Hilzer? How do you know this is true?"

"Well mother I may look like a lot of people but most of all I look like me. I figured you knew about this already."

"No, Holly why would I? How do you know Bert isn't your father?"

I have flashbacks when I hear certain tones, speech patterns, attitudes and phrases that are trademark things of my mother. They bring back very bad memories and feelings. Feelings that make me cringe inside. The tone of her voice over the phone was filling me with anger and disgust. Damn, I'm in a tight spot here so might as well just lay it all out. It was too late to attempt a cover up. Besides I had nothing to lose at this point. I was really surprised at that time that she was so seemingly shocked that Bert wasn't my dad. I really figured she knew.

Mandy had told her that I had known for 4 years and that I had proof. She went on to say that it was impossible that I wasn't Bert's daughter. Really, it was all just a pathetic attempt. I finally had to interrupt her very flawed defense as science trumps bull shit.

"Mom here's the deal" and I went on to explain to her about my blood type and the whole matter regarding the impossibility of Bert being my dad because his blood type is the only one that absolutely could not produce an AB Rh-negative baby. There is only one glitch to this and it has to do with being of Indian decent specifically Bombay India ... The Hilzers came from Prussia and the Jorgensens, my grandmother's family, were Dutch... I doubt any of them even ever saw a real Indian from India in their lives. So it was beyond doubtful that would have come into play.

Cat's out of the bag now and she is all kinds of riled up. In a way I was relieved and then scared. One thing I knew for sure was the already strenuous relationship I had with my mother had changed forever. All those years of denial, saying terrible things about Bert. Vehemently denying ever being unfaithful to him now was unequivocally disproven. I am the dirty little secret.

Before the conversation ended it was obvious to me she felt backed in a corner by her "save my own ass" efforts to tell me stories about how I was conceived.

Over the course of numerous texts to follow we again visited the subject of the blood types and I had to reiterate the impossibility of Bert being my father. She told me about how loveless her marriage to him had been and that she wanted to leave him but then he had his accident and she stuck around out of pity for him.

Prior to my birth, Bert was in a terrible construction accident that almost killed him. He was in a hospital in Denver for a long time and then spent 6 months in a Stryker bed at Craig Rehabilitation Center. According to my mother, as she was sitting in the hallway outside his room the night of the accident, a conversation took place between her and the doctor about how Bert would still be able to have kids, he'd just need help. It was a little more than I needed to know... The oddest thing about that part of her story was, why would that even be a subject of conversation about your husband, whom you had told me before you wanted to leave and divorce anyway? Come on, he's fighting for his life and you're talking about his ability to reproduce. REALLY? I listened as she went on to tell me that she thought after he recovered that a baby would fix things and so they had sex "his way" and then she inseminated herself. I will spare you the details as I wished she would have spared me. I tried to tell her that I didn't want to hear her story. My inner voice was screaming STOP!!! FOR THE LOVE OF GOD PLEASE STOP!!! I wanted to run. If there was ever a time I thought my mind was going to snap it was right then. It was all I could do to not put the phone down and walk out of my house on to the road and into traffic just so I wouldn't ever have to hear those words in my head again. Now that she said them they will forever be in my memory. I went from feeling like a beautiful human to feeling like discarded discharge shot from a turkey baster. It was gross and I was appalled; I found myself physically ill and I just wanted to puke and faint and wash my ears out with soap. Despite continuously saying I didn't want to hear anymore she kept going. It made me mad, not only was it a total bullshit story but apparently I was a batter baby, not even conceived normally.

I have no doubt she in fact, did what she said she did. But I surmise it was an act of desperate futility and an outlandish effort to cover up the careless result of an infidelity. I really think she believes her own story.

I spent the next nerve-grinding, emotionally exhausting few minutes explaining to her, again, what I had learned about blood types and how I got the records on Bert. When I could finally hang up I felt a moment of relief and then of dread. I knew then that was the reason why I couldn't ever move forward with the information I had. Dread, that feeling that encompassed the unknown and outcome that could not only wreck my life but others as well.

It was just pathetic and I was grateful when the call was over. I haven't spoken to her since that day. Texting is a different matter. There were lots of those and even though I changed phones I kept all of the texts and the letters that came in the mail. This time I wasn't going to destroy proof that she was toxic.

It is amazing what your mind will retain that can be called up from your memory. I don't remember so much about words as I remember events. Mostly, I remember the environment and whether it was happy or tension-filled. There were times growing up when I knew Bert was unhappy with Paul but never knew why. It didn't make sense until now. I remember overhearing arguments questioning my mother's fidelity and her always denying it.

Not long after the call I started getting more texts. My mother questioning and doubting and I thought genuinely remorseful. I was hopeful that she was going to help me. I actually thought that she was going to make things right. After a couple of days she texted me about my Uncle Paul; she said she wasn't proud of it but that she had an affair with him and that she would contact him about this. I was impressed. She was actually helping me. I had to give her his phone number but she did call him. It had been almost a year prior that my Aunt Judy, his wife, lost her battle to cancer and so her passing meant one less person that could be hurt by this. It was little consolation as they did have three grown children that still stood to be hurt. I didn't want to be the cause of upheaval. I didn't want to be that girl that steps over the happiness of others to serve her own end but this matter was out of my hands the minute Mandy told my mother that fateful night.

Apparently, my Uncle Paul was receptive to the situation. He was more shocked than she that they could have a child between them.   In a short time we hooked up on face book and eventually I asked him to do a DNA test. After some research and thinking time of his own he did consent, only after telling me that he had a vasectomy at some point during his fling with my mother.

 I wanted to fly to Denver to do it together. I wanted to see him provide the DNA so that there was no doubt that the results were valid. But instead he provided his DNA then sent the kit to me and I had my good friend, who is a nurse, take my DNA. I sent it off and then waited. I really thought that he would be my DNA dad. I couldn't imagine the outcome that was ahead of me.

 During the weeks that we waited for the results I felt very good about the fact that my mother seemed to want to help me to find my father. During our many texts she would express remorse and sadness that this had happened. I really thought she meant it. I was so sure that Paul was my dad. I looked in the mirror and saw attributes in myself that I could have easily gotten from him. I wondered how neat it would be to have 2 more half-sisters and a half-brother. I felt bad for them as what a shock I would be and then I even thought that if it were true that for their sakes it would maybe be better we just kept it between Paul and me. My track record with keeping secrets was unsurpassed and so just knowing would have been enough for me.

 My mother could not have been more apologetic and I just told her that I never felt like a mistake and that my existence was a blessing, that what mattered was that I was here. I believed it then and I believe it still; I believe it in spite of her and I never meant it as a way of condoning her trampy history but she would take it that way.

January 25, 2013,on a Friday evening as I sat next to Scott, each of us in our recliners side by side in the living room of our home. I was on my laptop when the email came through. Stalling wasn't going to solve anything so I sucked it up and opened the email; 99.99 percent that Paul was NOT my father. I was an expert at feeling numb by now, not shocked, not anything.

I sat for a few minutes as humor, my old friend, crept into my mind and I looked at Scott. Sounding like Ricky Ricardo I could only say "Lucy... you have some esplaining to dooooo!"

"DNA is Negative. Paul is not my father" read the text I sent my mother that night.

She texted back writing how I would always be Hilzer and that I was loved as a Hilzer and that I was always Bert's daughter. To me these words were patronizing and meaningless. Not to mention a bold faced lie. I was NOT Hilzer that much was proven. I had been raised to be a Hilzer my whole life. Proud of my family and our history, my kids were raised with that history. Now I was unclaimed, a bastard. Coming from a woman whose mental illness was stuck on convincing herself that everybody else had twisted reality and didn't live by the truth, now she was condoning that very thing. Slowly her own contradictions were slipping her up and showing her for the person she really was.

I was told this many times by those people, few that they were that even knew this was going on, my Aunt Joann, husband,

and sister. I know they only wanted to help. They didn't want to see me hurt so badly, but it just made things worse that they too chose to not face the reality. I lived the lie for 46 years and didn't know any better. Now I did and I wanted to know the truth. That's all I wanted was the truth. My kids had an idea of what was going on but all the details stayed between Scott and I even his family who means the world to me had no idea and to this day still have no idea.

My mother's next text to me stated that she was going to have to do some thinking to get things in chronological order.

My mind ran away with itself for the next few days. I heard rumors of her dating some mafia guy years ago and then there was just pure fantasy about how I could even be some lost heiress; I just felt she had the answers and that her delay in telling me was because she wanted to get in touch with the potential father figure before she spoke to me. This was most definitely not the case.

I tried to let things happen on its own. I didn't want to push things I was in no hurry to hurt more even though I wanted answers.

Then my mother finally texted, "I wish I could say it was rape, but it wasn't. He was very good-looking, well-to-do and married." She then went on to tell me that the tryst took place while she worked for a "high end" china and cutlery shop. To this day that is all I have to go on. She wishes she could say it was rape? Was that supposed to make me feel better? My self-esteem has already been shot through a turkey baster and now she wishes I was the product of a rapist? Well hell, that's the answer I was looking for that sounded much better. NOT!

With the texts that followed I tried to get more information from her. I really felt she knew more. All my attempts were met with obstinacy. Communication broke down quickly. One thing she is very good at is turning the tables on people. She quickly starts throwing my own words back at me, saying if I felt like a blessing and not a mistake why did it matter? I was Bert's daughter he loved me like his own. She had built a pathetic defense around herself and it was clear I wasn't going to get any further with her.

One thing for sure is that where my Dragon Queen mother is concerned I have learned my lesson. No more destroying the proof of her mental illness. In the past I threw out message machine recordings of her trying to coerce me with her verbal and psychological abuse, her motherly way of being nothing less than a bully - going to any extreme to serve her screwed up agenda. No more burning the letters and files containing her letters and proof of her betrayal. This time I kept the texts; I can't bear to reread them but I have them. In the following weeks and months I tried to gain her help and understanding asking her why she won't help me find my biological father. Her response always fell back on my saying I was a blessing either way - a comment I made when I was convinced Paul was my father. How could I ever have known it would end like this? That's what this comes down to for me. She was so helpful in the beginning and then when things didn't end up like she hoped it would, she finds some words to take out of context, words I said to help her feel better and she pathetically uses them as her armor against the truth. Her replies have been "It was 47 years ago, I can't remember his name." Gee thanks mom. So now I'm the end result of a lustful encounter between a slut and a cheating husband and father? You can't remember his name why? Was it because there were many moments of infidelity?

Another response I got from her was to look up Ray the Barber, a guy who used to cut Bert's hair and whom she was accused of having an affair with. She was extremely helpful with this tip as she even told me where his shop was located generally speaking, although it was 47 years ago. Again thanks Mom! For me this is the final betrayal of an egg donor. Harsh words, I know.

It is extremely hard for me to believe that this woman cannot remember my father's name. My mother is a very intelligent woman very cunning, calculative and manipulating. I know how she would research and do her homework when trying to figure out how to negotiate for herself on financial and legal matters. She does not lack resourcefulness. When Scott and I got married she actually tracked down a childhood friend who I had lost contact with years before to invite her to the wedding. That wasn't any small task. It just seems so odd that as smart as she is that she wouldn't know that with a little bit more information and the help of social media I could very possibly find my biological father. I can only assume there is a reason for why she doesn't want that to happen.

EIGHT

That night at my sister's place, we stayed up late and talked about everything. People and events my brother remembered that I had forgotten about or had become vague in my memory. He shared his own thoughts about our childhood. The brother I remembered was now a man I wanted to get to know better. I felt comfortable sitting there at the table talking and for once in my life I let my guard down. It didn't last for long. I was shocked the thought had even come up in my mind. The moment was surreal; I was actually contemplating telling them about something only a few people in this world knew. If I told them I would be committed to dealing with it in a way I wasn't sure I could face. Seriously, how do you tell your own siblings, that from the time you were an infant until you were 13 that your grandfather molested you? Is there ever a right time? There never seemed to be for me until lately.

Assessing the situation in my mind at that split moment I knew the reason why I wanted to tell them then was because the topic of our conversation was our grandfather and what a womanizer he was; more so than I ever knew. Brad knew and remembered so much more than I and some of what he spoke of sparked a vague recollection of the times. It also explained some things to me as to why the man I knew as my grandfather was the way he was. It never excused him for his behavior but what my brother spoke about brought some things full circle for me.

Brad's unbiased perspective about our grandfather made me feel like I could tell them about the things that had happened.

I couldn't do it. I didn't want to change the focus of our reunion. I didn't want to spend the time I had waited for so long to happen and the happiness and contentment I felt that was so foreign in my private life at the moment, rehashing such ugliness. I was content feeling that I could finally tell my story and it wouldn't be like taking an esteemed patriarch long since dead and dragging his good reputation through the mud.

More people stood to be hurt than I, if I were to ever have spoken of this before, people I loved and respected. I never mentioned a word about this growing up. So much was already going on in my family life and it never got any better the older I got. We were constantly dealing with family feuding waged by our mother against our father. In and out of court over matters that were totally blown out of proportion.

 All five of my mother's marriages where failures, one of which was to an alcoholic. A man who in a drunken stupor and no doubt reeling from her verbal acuity had taken a steak knife and threatened her life along with my unborn sister's as he held the knife to her belly. Had it not been for my brother pointing one of his loaded rifles at our stepfather and threatening to shoot him, things may have ended quite differently.

We seemed to be constantly moving; Idaho, California, and various cities in Colorado. All of these relocations happening before I was five years old, I remember them all.

That's just for starters. I knew even as a very young little girl that if I said a word about being molested that it would take my already dysfunctional existence and make it worse. People would become involved that I didn't want in my life. I stood to lose much more than I would gain.

When I was ten I learned to never trust anyone. I eluded to someone I thought was my friend that my grandpa was "friendly" with me. I made him promise not to tell and he did. I was lucky enough to wiggle out of it by saying he was lying and misunderstood me. The whole matter smoothed over quickly and nothing came of it. Sad that I even learned that lesson in that manner. How ironic that someone who cared for me tried to help me and did the right thing actually taught me to never trust anyone. My life was so fucked up but I could handle it the way it was.

"Grandpa, why do you play with me like that?"

"Ever since you were a baby you have always flirted with me. You've always been special."

 I can never remember a time before I turned 13 that I wasn't duck dive and dodging my grandpa Hilzer. It never made a difference to me when being able to spend time with Bert and the Hilzers. I would rather deflect and or relent to unwanted sexual advances from an old man than stay home with my mother.

As a very young girl I loved to drive my grandpa's pickup. At that time he and my grandmother had their farm in Briggsdale and I never missed the opportunity to go with him to check on the cows or drive into the COOP because that meant I could steer the pick-up. It was at these times that in my naiveté I would find myself in an unwanted situation.

 I always considered my grandpa to be a gentle giant. He was never overly forceful but still his tactics were effective for him. Had he been forceful and rough I have no doubt I would not be the person I am today. I'm not making excuses for him I'm just being plain honest. I learned to become a great bargainer although not always successful; paying for the privilege of being able to steer the pickup and eventually learn to drive it by giving into his part of the deal when I couldn't get out of it. As I got older instead of driving it was shopping and the older I got the better I was at deflecting his advances but again, not always successful. It was wrong but it was going to happen anyway, I knew that too.

I was always grandpa's girl, no one had any idea what was going on. I can't count the times. To be honest I really can't. My memories consist of having my pants pulled down turning my head and closing my eyes. I could go anywhere I wanted in my mind as long as I closed my eyes. It was just my body lying there on the truck seat or the freezer top in the storage room. As long as I closed my eyes the embarrassment of my own pudgy, imperfect body being naked and exposed was of no consequence because my mind was dreaming of being somewhere else. I knew what he was doing with his hands and his mouth but I couldn't feel it, trying to focus on my dream until somehow I could wiggle out of it after a few minutes.

By being uncooperative, eventually it would be over and a wave of relief would come over me. "Now maybe he will leave me alone for a while" I would think to myself. He would tell me if I ever told anyone he would go to prison. I knew that but it made no difference to me, what I cared about was that I seemingly felt I had some grasp on the relationship we had. I could always bargain with him and so the result of telling anyone would be nothing short of devastation to the life I had. Even though it sucked it was what I knew and I felt I could deal with it.

My grandfather going to prison was the least of my worries. However, being taken away and never seeing the Hilzers and being subjected to unwanted medical and social service people was not an option. At a young age I knew this would happen, I don't know how I knew but I knew, and it was unacceptable to me. (Maybe the idea came to me from watching too many talk shows.) I tolerated the advances and did the best I could to cope with them. I continued to endure the hip-gyrating when I would sit on his lap which to me was the most disgusting thing.

Despite the ugliness, I did love my grandpa very much growing up. The day he died I was inconsolable and relieved at that same time. It wasn't until way into adulthood, meaning more recently, that I began to view him for what he was, a very sick child molester that stole my innocence when I was still in diapers. Although it never got further than foreplay, thank God I bargained my way out of that till he died, I never considered myself ever being a virgin. It scares me to death to think that because I don't vividly remember every time, that my mind still has those memories tucked away and someday they will come back and it will take any sanity I cling to and stomp on it.

NINE

I had two glasses of wine and that was enough. I think Mandy could tell I was starting to get a little sick from it. Without a word said she brought me a glass of water. My gut was starting to do flip flops and contortion tricks, I just hoped I could tough it out without having to go lay down.

The conversation had moved on to our grandma Hilzer. She was a huge role model in my life. I adored her twinkling eyes and no one could beat her cooking. She put up with so much from our grandfather. I just never realized how much and it was that night that I realized why she would call him 'Nicholouse' instead of Nicholas. It also became clear to me that she must have known about his dealings with me. It would explain the times when she would watch me and certain ways she would treat me. I just thought she was being mean for no reason, but now I think it was because she suspected and yet wasn't going to say anything either unless I did.

Yet that woman taught me how to cook and sew and instilled things in my young life that I live by to this day. I was blessed to have her in my life for the first ten years and I thank God for that. It was because of her influence that I love to sew and create things. My very first sewing kit was a surprise gift from my mother before I was 5 years old. I loved to make clothes for my Barbie dolls and embroider. My first sewing machine was a little toy that used glue to "sew" fabric together.

From watching my grandma I learned to crochet. To this day I still remember the day she bought me my first skein of yarn from Woolco. I was spending part of my summer break with my grandparents and we had made the drive to Greeley from the farm in Briggsdale. Every two weeks we would come to town, it was an all day event and kind of a big deal. It was a long ride to town but going home was a different matter as I was the happiest kid in the back seat crocheting with my new hook and Red Heart skein of red yarn.

I was close to ten years old when my grandma decided I was old enough to understand how to read a sewing pattern. It was also my first official time shopping in a fabric store. Up until that day the only other place I loved to spend an afternoon in was the public library. Now I had two favorites, it was heaven being surrounded by all the color, all the possibilities of creating beautiful things. We chose a simple but cute pattern for a pullover tunic top. My grandma helped me figure out how much material we needed and where to read on the cover of the pattern for extra items we should buy.

Sharing that time with my grandma was priceless. I was excited and proud, standing at the fabric cutting table watching the lady cut the material we picked out.

My dad bought me my first grown-up sewing machine. A brand I've never seen since that day it was called a New Home. Compared to my grandmas PFAFF it was a hunk of blue metal with a needle. I learned how to use a sewing machine and all the basics on that old hunk. I even grew to love it and had it for several years, sewing lots of projects with it until my grandma passed away and I inherited her PFAFF. I still have the PFAFF; it has served me well and together we have sewn countless projects, quilts, clothes, Halloween costumes, Christmas presents everything and anything I could imagine.

In my hope chest I still have the first shirt I ever sewed. I went on to sew clothes for myself on my own even designing some as well. There is no doubt that this lady with the twinkling eyes shaped my world and by doing so gave me a creative outlet that I could focus on and express myself through.

TEN

As Brad slept on the couch it made me feel happy that after all these years he was just feet away from me. It felt good for the three of us to be together. Never in our lives had we had this chance and even though I still felt like a wreck inside I was trying to so hard to soak in every moment.

The three of us spent the next day just walking through old town Fort Collins. Brad and I picked on Mandy as we used to do and just enjoyed being together. I never wanted that day to be over. I had plans to go drive by places we used to live and old schools I attended. But this short time I was in Colorado was devoted to my brother and sister. I decided that I could Google Earth those places if I wanted to see them. Maybe right then wasn't the best time to do that. I had also thought about seeing my Aunt Joan and other family members in Denver. After our long night catching up I didn't think it was the right time then either. What's more I wasn't sure there would ever be a right time. The thought of not seeing them until one of them died saddened me, but the thought of being the focus of the visit in regard to the "who's my daddy"matter made me uncomfortable. So I prayed that God would hopefully see His way clear that someday before it was too late I might see these people and it wouldn't be such a difficult reunion.

To allow myself to live in the moment is hard to do. For me it means letting my guard down and not being concerned with the peripheral distractions. It means to not be so concerned with how fat I looked or how much of a farmbilly I would come off as, since I was so far away from my sanctuary. However, that day I did and I loved every minute of it. The day went by all too quickly; evening found us back at my sister's place, enjoying each other's company.

That night trying to hold back the tears I said goodbye to my brother. I felt that I would indeed see him again. A certain part of me was calmed down because he was in my life again. During the course of all our conversations I had pointed out that when you thought about the situation we were all only children. While we shared the same mother we each had a different dad. It moved our relationship to another level as did the years that had passed since we last saw each other. It made this new relationship kind of exciting; getting to know one another all over again a fresh start, kind of. It was marvelous and excruciating at the same time. That little voice deep down inside kept saying "Just don't screw this up Holly!"

Sunday morning 6:00 a.m. came too quickly because I didn't want to have to leave. I hadn't really slept that well the two nights I was there but that was all nerves. Throwing my overnight bag in the back seat I walked back into the house to say goodbye to Mandy, the kid sister that I never really got to know growing up. We lived under the same roof but we lived different hells. It would be wrong to say that her childhood was better than mine. She suffered with us and on her own. I may never fully know all that she has been through but she has hung in there.

Mandy has a knack that is hard to explain. She is quirky and yet perceptive. She has a way of bringing things together in an unconventional manner. I can't really do her justice in fully explaining my little sister. She is trying really hard to get her life together and to be a better person every day, much like we all are. She is on her own for the first time in 14 years and it's all new to her. She has my respect and I love her dearly and what's more I am indebted to her for bringing Brad back into my life. As I hugged her before I left, I really hugged her. Hoping that she could feel all the love and gratefulness I felt for her just by that one hug. My eyes became a waterfall of tears and I looked her in the face and thanked her for bringing us all together and told her that it meant more to me than she would ever know. None of the last couple of days would ever have been possible without her. It was then that I made the personal promise to myself to be a better big sister to her; not that I was terrible; I wasn't a great one either.

I didn't know who my real father was but I did know who my kid sister and big brother were and I was going to be a better sister to them. With that thought I got in my car and pointed it towards home. So much was running through my mind that I knew the next 600 miles or so would be devoted to putting the puzzle pieces together of what I already knew and what I had just learned.

ELEVEN

I hate crying it makes my eyes puffy and my head hurt and it weakens my exterior. I grew up crying and then I just learned to not allow myself to cry. It worked well for me for years, if being insensitive and tough works for you. Looking back from the very beginning to present day it is one thing that I still have done my fair share of. Praying is another. Crying for some people is a release. For me when I cry it brings back all the hurt and I can feel it welling up inside me. It's the hurt I have carried with me all these years. I have tried to unload the baggage as one of my favorite Christian writers, Max Lucado, would write of only to find it to be temporarily successful. I have tried real hard to not carry this baggage in my life. So many questions that are unanswered, some I am very scared of never knowing the answer. Before my life hit the skids this last time I thought I had everything in a place where I could deal with it and move on. I know beyond a doubt that had this been handled differently by my mother I wouldn't be so scared and feel so lost.

I have spent a great deal of my life trying to fit all the pieces together that tell the story of me. The question of my parentage now changes everything about me. The man I knew as my dad knew he probably wasn't my father yet raised me as his own. I grew up thinking I was a Hilzer and that was a big part of my life and a big deal to me. Now I find out that's a lie. It also changes the feelings I had about my grandfather molesting me. He went from being my grandfather to being some dirty old man in my mind as the other people who I thought I was related to now have become very kind strangers who loved me. The family I was least attached to, the Henry's, now ironically became the only family I am related to.

The mother who started out seemingly being helpful about all this has returned to her old self, guaranteeing that only by the grace of God will I ever find out who my dad is. I've come to believe that the reason why the whole molestation experience hasn't had near the impact in my life as the incredible amount of hurt my mother has is because I could have at any time changed the course of those events. With one peep from me that old man would have spent the rest of his life in prison. I knew what the outcome was going to be for the both of us and I was smart enough to know that I didn't want that to happen. My silence became worthwhile to me. I had already lost my innocence before I even knew what it was and so it was too late for me in that regard. However, He was going to pay for his action that was God's department, not mine. To my family I was the most spoiled grandchild in truth it was deeper than that. I had reckoned with the devil in a way.

 Because of the embarrassment of my own body I was never promiscuous growing up. I partied and had a lot of fun when I was old enough to go out or sneak out. But I was never a slut. I did what I had to do to survive and I know I made the right decision not to tell.

TWELVE

There were many conversations that took place where my brother and I would tell our dad about what it's like to live at home and how our mother acted. He knew how she could be, he was married to her. Bert never said a bad word about her until my brother and I were adults. Even then what he would say was tame in comparison to what she said about him. Bert always tried to encourage us to keep a relationship with our mother despite her tongue. I remember one time he told me that when she wanted to be she was a great lady. I knew what he meant because I had seen that side of her as well it's the unpredictable behavior and attitude that was the problem.

The courts had long since let my brother and me down. It was the late 70's early 80's; things like psychological, emotional and verbal abuse weren't the catch phrases of the day yet. Those terms weren't recognized in any way. It wasn't physical abuse but it still hurt just as much. My brother and I would try to talk with our mother about the fact that sometimes it wasn't what she said so much as how she said it. She had a way with talking that could take a simple word like 'hi 'and say it so that you shuddered when you heard it. She was and still is a master of manipulation and this is one of her specialties. We tried on numerous occasions to get her to understand but each time ended up in an escalation of emotions. She would raise her voice a little and then we would have to raise ours a little so she could hear us over her own voice. She had what I call her trademark phrases and words that to this day I cringe when I hear them the memories attached to them are ones of feeling like I'm beyond ever being understood and trapped.

That's really what us three kids were, trapped. We were too little to be able to do anything but endure her hatefully sarcastic venomous tongue and her flip flop personality. I tried so very hard for the most part of my life to gain her understanding and to finally find that place of acceptance. Each time it was like she couldn't help herself and something would happen to ruin it.

Parenting is serious business. I wholeheartedly believe that as parents we are 100 percent responsible to our children for the good and the bad. But they are 100 percent responsible for being better humans because of or in spite of their parents.

My dad would say you will never know if you've done a good job in life till you're dying and you look back; you'll never know how you did as a parent until then. I really don't think my mother's father or mother could say they did a good job. Even as a kid I could tell that she longed for something from her father. Maybe it was the same thing I longed for from her. After all, how could one give something they never had?

Despite being the product of questionably bad parenting she still had the power to change things for the sake of her own kids. She still had the ability to not repeat those same pitfalls. I think on some level she tried, but I also believe it was her behavioral impairment that always got in the way. I'm not making excuses for her; I'm just trying to be fair. She still brought insurmountable hurt to bear on my life, yet there were some good times as well. For the sake of ever being hurt again, or having my children hurt again, I can't have anything to do with her. I forgive her and I pray for her. I sincerely hope her life is as full as it can be. But I have to insulate myself, when the question of my parentage came to light that was the last straw. I wonder if that makes me a bad Christian, I hope not, if so all I can do is pray for forgiveness.

THIRTEEN

I was 18 when I met my husband. I had moved away from my mother's grasp when I was 16 and was living with my dad. 1985 meant you could be 18 and still go to a 3.2 bar and drink beer. I was a senior attending high school in the day and a community college at nights, studying to become a certified public accountant. I dreamed of the possibility of someday working on Wall Street. The idea of money, freedom and power was appealing to me. The night I met Scott I ditched my college class with a friend and we went to the bar. Our courtship really wasn't one. As a matter of fact our whole dating experience was completely nontraditional. Our story isn't a sappy sweet romantic story. Angels didn't sing, bells didn't ring and if cupid shot his arrow it was poisoned dipped first. We were total opposites; to say we were a million to one shot deal would be an understatement. Maybe all this is exactly why we succeeded at being married for 29 years now.

Our time together started out rather unconventional and really to this day still is. Scott came from large family whose folks had to work hard to keep a roof over their heads. The Cronk's where Missouri natives, everyone born and raised in Maryville Missouri.

 If I had to say what one thing stood out the most about Scott was that he had the kindest blue eyes I ever saw. When I looked in them I saw goodness. I knew it was there even if he didn't which explains the bad boy edge he had as well. I wasn't looking for a long term relationship so we started out with a no strings attached understanding. Shortly after we moved in together, which was about 3 weeks after we met, that all pretty much went out the window.

Bert was pissed when I told him I was moving in with Scott. I think looking back he was worried and scared more. I will never forget what he told me the day I moved out. "You will never be any better than your mother. You will shack up with one guy after another." Harsh words but I knew he was hurt and I promised myself that wasn't going to be the case. I never cared to look around or do any more 'boy' shopping so to speak.

Our first home was a single wide trailer that was probably built way before either of us was born. Not the most energy efficient but it was the perfect party pad and love nest. We partied and had fun at night and the weekends. During the week Scott worked and I went to school. I had quit my college classes and just had high school to attend by this time. Scott was a labor hand for a pipeline company. He was just starting out but he knew what he wanted to do and he went for it. Days turned to months and I graduated from high school and we decided we wanted to travel, so we did.

June of 1985, I was free as a bird. Despite Bert's warning that I would never graduate from high school, I still did. I think he said the things he did because he knew it would make me more resolute to not end up like he spoke of, I'm not really sure. Whatever the reason for the things he said they were never taken by me as being mean or hateful. I knew he was scared for me. I knew he worried about my brother and I.

Bert was the first man I ever respected. He was my rock and pillar of strength and positivity. The only other man I respected as much as and more than my dad was Scott.

The very first pipeline job Scott and I went on was in Hobbs, New Mexico. We drove overnight to get to that job, a caravan of cars crossing Colorado through Trinidad and down into New Mexico. We had partnered up with a buddy of Scott's and another guy we used to call Lame Ron. I think the name is self-explanatory. Scott drove my Toyota Celica loaded with our stuff and Thor. I drove our buddies T-Top Trans Am. It was a night crossing so we would stop periodically to do a line of speed and then motivate on. Late in the night we drove through a little desert town that had a beauty parlor. I'll never forget that little shop because prominently advertised in its front window was "Blow-Jobs $2.00". Thank God the guys didn't see that or we would have been waiting for the shop to open the next morning.

We found a huge house to rent that had a big yard for Thor to run in and three clothes lines that spanned the back yard from end to end. Sadly, the yard was full of sand thorns and so poor Thor didn't do all that much running. However, the clothes lines got put to good use. Hobbs was a dry county, no alcohol could be sold. It was a 45 minute road trip to the county line where we could buy booze and lucky for us the same guy also sold pot. It was a sad house when we were running short on money as that meant no booze and no party favors. It also meant we ate a boat load of hot dogs. Thank God for pay days!

My days were filled with laundry and waiting for Scott to get home. I did drive around and check the town out, all in all Hobbs was a nice town. I remember being so surprised that after a huge rain storm there was no mud, as everywhere you looked it was all sand so everything seemed to dry out immediately.

Eventually, the living quarters got a little cramped. The days were long in the New Mexico heat; Scott would come home exhausted so after supper we'd go to bed. I remember lying there with him, his arms around me, they offered assurance that everything was going to be ok as long as we had each other. Our bodies fit snugly against each other like we were one being. I trusted him with my heart and unquestionably my safe keeping even though he was only 19.

After a month or so it became obvious that we couldn't stay in the house we rented with our friends and we really couldn't afford a place on our own so we loaded up the Celica and the three of us, Scott, me and Thor headed home.

Pipelining is a rough and rowdy life. It's difficult to describe to someone who lives an 'ordinary' kind of life. We were very much like hired guns. We worked for the contractor that had the biggest job. We were ready at a minutes' notice to travel to anywhere that a job was kicking off.

To be clear this was the natural gas and oil industry. All over the United States there is a gridlock of gas and oil pipelines. They criss cross each other and they go over and under each other. They span gullies and valleys and are even bored under roads and through rivers. Societies Ken and Barbie have no idea that behind the scenes of every life convenience they enjoy on a daily basis is an ugly truth of how it comes to be.

Home was a 20ft cobra pull type trailer that was my grandparents at one time. Home was the Wagon Wheel Motel in Dumas, Texas. Home was a large house in Hobbs New Mexico that we shared with our friends that we pipelined with.

Home, had a different definition for us. Home was anywhere Scott and I were together, simple as that.

Pipelining is one of the most dangerous occupations I know. Ditches cave in, tractors roll over, things blow up, and people die. Every morning Scott and the guys woke up facing this and the fact that they came home at night was cause for some celebration. Everyone in those days partied. Smoke some pot, do a little speed, drink some whiskey and shoot the bull. I could tell you stories that would make your hair curl.

Sometimes we didn't get any sleep at all. Seven days a week we worked as much as 18 hours a day. We were young and rowdy. We were bullet proof and we had no responsibilities other than to each other, and our pit bull Thor.

If I wasn't fortunate enough to work in the field office doing payroll or running supplies, my time was devoted to seeing that Scott was taken care of and any of the other guys who just needed someone to do their laundry, sew their buttons and handle their business matters for them.

Everyone had a click or group they hung with. It was like a bunch of little communes we would stay together or stay close to each other. We barbequed at night or shared our delicious concoctions that spent the day back in our rooms simmering in a crock pot. We drank and partied and when the job was over we said our goodbyes and maybe down the road we'd run into each other on another job.

Pipelining was an adventure and we had a blast. A lot of shenanigans took place. Life is precious; we didn't show our respect for that fact living the way we did. You are only young once and I would do it all over again. It was a time of my life that I just lived for the first time, it was wild, and it was crazy.

We had money, we had fun, and we did incredibly stupid things and lived through it. DAMN! What a ride that was!

Drugs were the party favor. Pot, all kinds and any kind besides ditch weed, of course. Speed, preferably cocaine or crank and booze; Budweiser or whiskey, the good stuff, crown royal, Jim Beam and some Jack. If one of us had some, all of us had some.

It wasn't always fast times, eventually a job would get finished and we would pack up and split for the next job or head home for a break or in hopes of getting hired on locally until another big job kicked off. Greeley, as much as I disliked the town, was home base. Family ties meant more so this is where we always returned to.

FOURTEEN

The fall of 1985 we had just come off a job and along with some of our friends we rented out spaces at the KOA campground just east of Greeley. Scott and our buddies got hired on with a local pipeline company we'd worked for before. I spent my days hanging out with the girlfriends, going to visit my mom at work, grocery shopping, cooking and just taking care of Scott. I loved taking care of him. He worked hard and I really liked making sure he had clean clothes, hot meals and a beer waiting for him when he got home. I never minded being called his old lady... Then it was cute. Now that I am old it isn't.

Our little camper only had small propane tanks on it so getting them filled all the time was a pain. Frequently we relied on body heat, including that of our canine companion, and love to stay cuddly warm through the nights. The beginning of October that year was brutally cold. I wasn't working and had embroidered everything I could think of; in short I was stir crazy.

Scott and I had been inseparable since March, less than nine months. Marriage had been a passing thought for me but I never said a word to Scott. I never had a pre-determined way of how I dreamed of being proposed too. The bended knee thing was too overboard for me. This was a good thing for Scott as my low expectations were exceeded when his proposal was,

"So, when are we going to get married?"

My reply was "When Hell froze over!"

I wanted to elope but we both knew our mothers would be hurt if we did. Neither of us wanted any pomp or circumstance, we weren't about having all the attention on us. I definitely wasn't a bridezilla that had to have her special day be perfect. The main thing I cared about was getting married by a preacher in a church and not some judge.

It took some finagling to get that done because we had decided on October 26th as our day; we had two weeks to plan.

My mother was in overdrive. At first she tried to convince me to wait a year but I would have none of it. My father, Bert, probably realized I was going to do what I wanted so he gave us his blessing. Although, I know it was with apprehension and understandably so.

I found the church, the preacher and the dress. My little sister was my bridesmaid and other than that I didn't care about anything else. My Mother was instrumental in getting invitations printed and mailed. She made plans with Scott's mom and of course Bert. She also hosted a bachelorette party for me. I know she did these things because she wanted more for me than I cared about having. It was sweet and I appreciated everything she did.

Scott and I had to finance our weddings bands. We choose two simple gold bands with small scalloped edges. I never cared for big ass diamonds. I'm not sure what the history is with buying huge baubles for engagement and wedding rings. They prove nothing to me other than a waste of money that could be better spent on a home or future. It was the love that mattered to me. I have diamonds and sapphires and such but my favorite ring is and always has been that simple gold wedding band.

Scott and I were married on a Saturday at Noon on a beautiful fall day. My mother's apartment was just a block from the church. I had spent the morning there with her and my sister getting ready for the big event. It was a beautiful walk to the church and when the building came to view I was surprised to see that Scott had already arrived. The minute I saw his truck parked in front was the minute it hit me this was for real. I kind of half expected him to be late or not show up I don't know why, it really would have been out of character for him. Maybe it was my own insecurities that were running wild.

I was happy to see my aunts and their families there. I always felt miniscule to others and I never thought I meant enough to them to have them come even at short notice. My cousins and extended members were all there. It meant the world to me that they came. They probably thought it was no big deal, I did.

The Henry side was represented by my grandparents and an aunt and uncle. Even though they were invited by my mother I knew they only came for the looky-lou aspect of things. When the ceremony was over they didn't stick around long enough to say a word to me. They slipped out the back door, unnoticed but not before leaving their gift of two cheap plastic candle holders with matching candles. It's the thought that counts and I knew they did more for their other grandchildren. Personally I didn't want them there nor did I care about the present. It was the fact I believe to this day they only came to gather information to gossip about. My mother and I were very sure that the Henry family gossip was that the reason why we got married so hurriedly was because I was pregnant. It gave me great satisfaction to disprove that as it would be almost five years before any babies would come along.

Scott's parents and most of his immediate family were in attendance. His dad had driven all night in the truck to get there but he made it. He was in the church long enough to see us get hitched and then he went and napped in their car.

It was a quick ceremony, Bert didn't want to walk me down the aisle, I believe primarily because of his legs. I don't think he wanted attention drawn to his handicap. So Scott and his brother and my sister just walked to alter. I asked the preacher to read the basic vows, including the love, honor and obey part. I believe in traditions, I believe in women being women and men being men, I believe that if you love a man enough to marry him than you must also trust in him too. If you trust in him than you know he would never ask of you without considering your viewpoint in doing so. It was an all or nothing deal for me.

Having said I do we were now man and wife. I was a proud Mrs. Scott Cronk. As I hugged my dad he said one thing to me. "Make it last a lifetime." I promised him I would.

As a wedding present my parents gave us money to rent a really nice trailer house in the same park we rented our first home earlier that year. It was on a nicer side of the trailer park and it was a great start for two kids. We spent our first Thanksgiving and Christmas in that trailer. It was nice being in the same place for what seemed to us as a long time. I spent my time making our trailer a home and being a wife. Scott worked for a local company and on occasion would snow out and get to stay home. It took a lot for a pipeline job to shut down for any reason so we really enjoyed the rare time it would happen. We'd get stoned, watch movies and chase each other around the house. We were just kids, I was still only 18, he turned 20 already and we were in love.

 Our youthfulness worked for us and against us. It worked for us in that we didn't know any different than what we had and against us in that emotionally I expected more from Scott at times that guys just don't tune-in to. Thanksgiving was one of those times. It was our first huge fight, one sided as Scott failed to see any cause for discord but I did, even though I don't remember the reason. As we walked from our truck to my mother's front door I remember turning back to him and saying, "I hate you! I wished I had never married you!" I didn't mean it; I just wanted his feelings hurt like mine were.

It didn't work as his response was, "You'll get glad in the same shoes you got mad in."

 This made me even madder. How was I going to argue with that? As it turned out he was right. One of my favorite pictures of us is me sitting on his lap just a couple hours later in my mom's living room.

Our first Christmas was not without turmoil either. My mother had loaned us one of her fake trees. A real pretty white snow flocked tree. It was gorgeous all decorated in our living room. The twinkling lights, the tree skirt I made with our name on it. All the presents I beautifully wrapped. I was so proud the house was all decorated everything was perfect. Except that our trusty companion Thor loved the tree so much he peed on it. The white snow was yellow snow and I had to rewrap the presents. This didn't happen just once. It happened repeatedly; I had no support from Scott on the matter. He was oblivious to the entire ordeal his dog was putting me through. So after a week the tree came down, I cleaned it up fixed the flocking and put it back in the box. Scott got his pee soaked underwear and other presents I had gotten him still covered with Thor's contribution and that was the end of our first Christmas.

FIFTEEN

Pipeline jobs close to home where getting few and far between so after the first of the year Scott started working for my dad. Bert had managed a road construction company now since the mid 1970's. I grew up around construction. I was the boss's daughter and could hold my own. Although the times I would go to work with my dad only included spending the day in his office or in his truck with him, if we had to go out on location. I still learned a lot watching him do his job. The guys respected him, so did Scott. Between road patching, sawing and sealing concrete highways and airport tarmacs my dad kept Scott busy.

At one point I was able to go on site with Scott. They had just put down new concrete on Interstate 70 coming out of Denver heading into the mountains. It was a big job and meant really late hours. We had to wait for the concrete to cure enough to saw the joints on the slab. It would be two or three in the morning before we could start sawing. Scott would run the saw and I would hussle the hose and move the water truck as he would work his way down the Interstate. It would be just him and I out there. There would be cars, big trucks and limos whizzing by all night long, it was hard work but I had fun. I loved working with Scott.

When we had the chance to cut loose it was usually at our buddy's house just down the road from where we lived. We'd all get together on the weekends and get rowdy and roughhouse. The rowdy part wasn't a problem and usually neither was the roughhouse part except for one night.

Our buddy had just bought the house next to his and was going to fix it up and rent it. We ended up having a house warming party in it that turned into a wrestling match. That evening I had enough partying and went home early. Irritated that Scott didn't choose to leave with me I drove home with a buzz and flopped into bed. The next thing I know his mom is sitting on the edge of the bed trying to wake me up. Scott was in the emergency room and needed a ride home. I told her, "let him drive himself home". He couldn't because he was banged up. So I got dressed and went to the hospital. After a short wait here came my betrothed puffy face and all. He had a broke his jaw and was walking with a sever limp. I was still stewing mad from the events earlier in the evening so I had no sympathy for him or his condition. If he wanted a ride home he better keep up.

Waking up the next morning I was still fuming over the matter. Apparently he had driven to the house and tried to wake me to take him to the hospital but in my sleep stupor I told him to drive himself. I didn't feel an ounce of remorse over it. As far as I was concerned if he had come home with me he wouldn't be in the fix he was.

We had no health insurance and he needed to see an oral surgeon about his jaw. The first guy we saw wanted cash up front. He was a dickhead anyways. The funny part about seeing this guy was that there was a long set of stairs to get to his office. I remember getting out of the truck and smiling as I looked at the stairs. I had no problem walking up them but Scott did and I spared him no mercy.

Luckily, Scott's mom knew a dental surgeon that would take care of him. He ended up with his jaw tied shut for ten weeks. I eventually got over being pissed and spent the next weeks buying baby food for him to suck down and making fun of his speech and gimpy walk.

 Scott continued to work for my dad while his jaw was in traction. Eventually his co-workers learned to understand him. He was already tall and lean so the forty pounds he lost left him looking like a prisoner of war.

 At one point he was so hungry for a cheeseburger that we pureed one with fries in the blender. It wasn't as appetizing as he hoped for. It got a little frustrating when I couldn't decipher what he was saying but I never missed the opportunity to make light of his situation.

 At the end of his torture I was in the room when he woke up from having his jaw untied. His first words were, "Hi Baby." All I could think of was... My God he has an accent! I never noticed it before. Our friend's homeowners insurance paid two thousand of the bill, the rest we got left on the hook for. This wasn't the first dumb ass thing we'd got ourselves into and it wouldn't be last.

SIXTEEN

Scotts 21st birthday was that following August. We had been busy working for my dad all summer so I was excited to plan a weekend camp trip to celebrate the special day. I baked and decorated a cake, bought the booze and packed the cooler and camping gear. I picked him up from the job site at quitting time and we headed straight to our favorite spot in the mountains.

We spent three glorious days fishing, tramping around the Rockies, getting stoned and being newlyweds. I was so proud of the birthday cake I made for him and was so excited for him to see it. Sadly, it met an untimely demise as while we were setting camp up I placed it on our cooler which was not on level ground. The cake, protected in a Tupperware container, rolled off the cooler and down the hill right next to the river we were camped by. I chased after it but by the time I got to it the container had finished rolling and fell on its bottom. The cake inside looked like it took a ride in the blender. Well, I thought, it may not be pretty anymore but it will still be yummy. So I carried it back to camp put it on the now leveled cooler and we went fishing.

Supper time came and then dessert. Having the munchies I was really craving some birthday cake. When I took the lid off of the cake it was covered in ants that had already been enjoying our sweet treat. I almost considered shaking the ants off and still eating a piece but common sense over ruled the thought and so we never got to enjoy the masterpiece I spent so much time decorating. All these years later we still talk about the cake that was. Living it was a very comical experience. No matter how good a writer I am, I could never fully describe how funny we looked, two stoned kids chasing a cake down the rocky hill.

SEVENTEEN

Later that fall, having finished the job my dad's company had, we were faced with living off of unemployment at the house or accepting a job offer and going on the road again. It was a no brainer so in three days I had the house packed up. All the things we wouldn't need and couldn't take with us were put in storage and we were on our way to Bethany, Missouri. Scott was going to do something different than pipeline. This time it was a water treatment plant, not the ideal job but it paid well and we had nothing else on the hook.

Our first wedding anniversary came around while we were on that job. The momentous occasion was celebrated with a weekend in Kansas City and a fun day at the Worlds of Fun amusement park. Hanging in our living room still, is an 'olde time' picture we had taken on that day. I was dressed in a floppy hat and wedding dress and Scott was handsomely wearing a cavalry soldier's uniform. That picture has a lot of meaning to us both. I was only 19 at the time; we were still kids but already had done so much in our short time together.

For four years that's how we lived, traveling to Oklahoma, New Mexico, Missouri, Texas, Colorado, Utah, and Wyoming, going where the work was. Scott and I just had each other, it was us against the world. We worked hard played hard and no matter what we were always a team.

After finishing a Job in Dumas Texas we had a bank roll saved up and so we traded up and bought a new fifth wheel trailer and truck to pull it with. This was our home on wheels for a couple of years. When we would come off of a job we would always come home to my dad's place, and park it there. In between jobs Scott would help Bert do whatever, project he had planned out and I would take care of the trailer house we called home base. I'd cook and clean and take care of my guys.

Years before when my grandma died she left my grandfather and dad behind to fend for themselves. Not that they couldn't handle it but I stepped up and took on the roll whenever I stayed with my dad. After my grandparents sold their farm in Briggsdale they moved to what was marketed as an upscale mobile home park. It really started out being a very nice neighborhood to live in. Hill-n-Park was what it was called. Unfortunately, for the dry arid land that it set upon, sand thorns where terrible and they over took the nice park that once was there as well as everywhere else they could overrun. That was the worst part about that place.

I was very little when they sold their farm but I remember that time in my life. When my grandparents moved to town they also brought with them my great grandmother Jorgensen. She was my grandma's mother. Great grandma Jorgenson was a sweet old lady. I never really knew her very well. But I remember that much. She had an all white kitty named Snowball and the two of them lived in a trailer as well. Her trailer was moved from the Hilzer farm to Greeley so that she could remain close to my grandparents. They were neighbors at Hill'n Park. When my great grandmother passed away my dad sold his restaurant in Empire Colorado and bought her trailer.

One of my most favorite times growing up was spending time with our dad while he owned the Hard Rock Café in Empire Colorado. It was the perfect little town tucked away in the mountains. Empire enjoyed a fair share of tourism but for the most part was a sleepy little town. My dad had his living quarters behind the restaurant part of the building and the town dance hall was above us. The lower level had a walk out and it was this area that my dad used as his shop and where he spent time working on his gunsmithing projects. My brother was old enough to work for my dad in the kitchen so he made a few bucks being the chief dishwasher. I got to help the cooks.

Every Wednesday was cinnamon roll day. It was my favorite day as the lady that came to make the rolls let me help roll out the dough and put all the yummy fillings on it before we rolled it back up, cut them and left them to rise. I was always a chubby kid and having access to anything I wanted to eat anytime of the day really didn't have the impact you'd think it would. It was still very cool to be able to order anything I wanted.

I had a little friend that lived locally and so my days were spent helping the cooks, playing with my friend, riding her Shetland pony and browsing the little shops in town. My dad set up a charge account for me at the little grocery and curio store. They had the best trinket and toy section. For a little eight year old girl the one and only isle that was adorned with dime store toys was like a treasure chest for me. It had the best selection of ten cent rings any girl could ever hope for and I could get as many as I wanted.

My dad kept a pool table and a couple of foosball tables at the restaurant. While I loved to play, my brother was better than I. We would spend afternoons having foosball tournaments with the locals. The kitchen and waitress staff we had was like family to us so when business was slow the game was on. Listening to the juke box play the Allman Brother's, Ramblin

Man and Rod Stewart's Maggie, time seemed to fly by. It was the early 1970's and for this bouncy pigtailed little girl the living was great.

The surrounding mountains seem to stand like guardians over this sleepy little town. Year around scenery was pristine and beautiful. An occasional tour bus would stop in; sometimes we would have snow bunnies that had to detour through Empire because of road closures in the winter. It was this time in my life that my love for the wilderness and the Rockies blossomed. When my dad sold the restaurant I was broken hearted but the flip side was that he would be closer. I still think of those days and all the happy times I had there.

Nothing lasts forever and so years after when I lost my grandma that's how it came that I began to cook for my dad and grandfather. I was only ten and yet here I was with a grocery list and a grandpa with a checkbook. Together we would go grocery shopping. Naturally, for a price, I got to drive to the city limits than my grandfather would take over. I used coupons and looked through the sale flyers even then. Although coupons weren't as big as they are now. However, I do remember double and even triple coupon days; those were the best times to go shopping.

 Those poor guys, I would have recipes and with just the little bit of kitchen education I received from my grandma before her death, I was able to cook some pretty atrocious dinners. But they gutted it down. I Learned early on that recipes come with directions for a reason and when your ten years old it's better to follow them. I cleaned my dad's place when my brother and I would come to visit. I actually looked forward to taking care of them.

From the time I was very little I have always sewed and crocheted. I designed clothes for my babies and baby dolls and I loved fashion design. I loved to create things even before I knew that's what it was. As a little girl already dealing with so much privately I look back now and I realize it was the smiles on the faces of the people I loved that made me want to make things and do things for them. It made them happy if I gave them something. It pleased them that I took after my grandmother in so many ways. It was an honor to be compared to her and still is. When she passed it seemed like it was my place to pick up the reigns. It wasn't expected of me, no one forced this on me, I just did. It was a great experience for me and I am grateful for it. It says a lot about how nurturing overall the Hilzer's were. They were not without their flaws. They were human after all, but to me they were everything. My aunts, my uncles, and my cousins not a one of them ever judged me. Our time together most every Sunday had such an impact on my life that without that I know I would have been worse off.

Sunday family dinner was the highpoint of my life. The Hilzer's would all gather and as my grandma and aunts cooked, my grandfather, dad and uncle would be puttering around. Us kids my brother and three other cousins would be riding mini bikes around the park or we'd be taking turns getting pulled around on an inner tube with the snowmobile in the winter. There was always something going on.

The only thing that topped our Sunday dinners was the annual Hilzer family reunion. It was always great fun to have everybody together. Being young I didn't know many of them but they all knew who my brother and I were. There was always a keg of beer and tables lined up filled with homemade goodies. When we got tired of having our cheeks pinched we would go investigate the rodeo arena at the park. This was where the Greeley Stampede was and still is held every year. If we could squeeze between or under the gates we would walk around the empty arena. Otherwise my brother and I always stayed close to our father. I don't remember all the names but I do remember lots of smiling faces lots of hugs lots of laughter and hearing lots of stories. I loved to hear stories about my family and how they homesteaded and their journey to America. It was living history and it gave me roots in this world that I was proud of growing up.

EIGHTEEN

When Scott and I would come back to Greeley we looked forward to being with my dad. He never let his physical limitations interfere with what he did in life. That man suffered a great deal of physical pain till the day he died. We almost lost him twice to blood poisoning due to infections from injuries he sustained on his paralyzed legs. He never once complained about his predicament. He had no tolerance for those who whined about life when they were able bodied. When people would ask how he was Bert would always reply, "Warm and vertical."

Here was a man that wasn't expected to live and then was told he'd never walk again. That he'd be in a wheel chair the rest of his life, yet he did walk. Using a crutch and cane he basically dragged his lower body with him everywhere he went.

Nothing kept this man from living, time and time again he showed this by example. If he wanted to build something he figured out how to do as much of it on his own as possible. He built his woodshop and a boat from scratch. If his roof leaked he figured out how to get himself up a ladder and on the roof to fix it.

My brother and I had such respect for him that we would walk alongside of him or slightly behind him. We walked as if that was our usual pace in line with him when in fact we could have easily left him behind.

When my dad would pick us up to stay with him, most times when I was very little it involved a trip to Kmart for some toys for me to play with. He and my brother worked on guns and projects along those lines, my interests involved Barbie Dolls. I had everything Barbie. On one particular trip to Kmart my indecisiveness resulted in this poor man pushing a buggy up and down the Barbie Doll isles not just once but countless times. I had the luxury of being able to get anything I wanted and there was so much to choose from.

Bert placed his cane in the buggy part and used his free hand to push while he kept his crutch for balance and leverage. As I paced the isles he shuffled them. Eventually he had to make the decision for me. His solution was that he grabbed not one but two Barbie dolls so I had twins and then he went to where the Barbie clothes were displayed and cleaned off the racks filling the buggy. I had the best dressed Barbie's ever! For a little girl this was a dream come true. It wasn't until years later that memory stopped being about how spoiled I was and became about the limits to which he went for his kids. It wasn't easy for him to drag himself and to somehow push a buggy as he chased a chubby little girl back and forth in the toy isle. But he did it with patience and love.

I think that says it all. When the saying life's a bitch was popular... it never caught in his house.

 Bert in many ways taught me how to be a good woman and I hope a decent human being. He never taught me to be subservient, he never expected me to be the little lady. While I loved my Barbie's I also loved riding the mini bike and snowmobile. I shot guns and had my own. I did a lot of boy stuff. I took shop class and the hunter safety course. Mostly just to prove that I could do them better and still wear a dress. I loved showing him my welding projects. My enthusiasm was fueled by his praise. I did learn that knowing how to cook and keeping a clean house pleases a man. I learned that you must always try to be the better person. That if the day came and you didn't like what you saw in the mirror that was your own damn fault. Respect, integrity and honor are core traits. Naturally, growing up I slipped a little here and there. But I never forgot.

I remember I was near my 20's and Scott and I were home for a short time. I was old enough now that the conversations I would have with Bert were more adult to adult and not father to child. He once told me that I should use my mother as an example of how not to be. It was the best piece of advice anyone has ever given me. I strive for that in everything to this day.

Some conversations I couldn't bear to be a part of. He was facing his own mortality and I was oblivious to that fact. Those conversations about his final wishes and having made peace with God were hard for me to handle. The thought had never occurred to me that I would ever be without my dad. Yet when I tried to envision him later in life I could never imagine him white haired and aged. Looking back I know he knew his time was running short and he was trying to prepare me. He once told me that he knew I would be alright because I had Scott. But that he worried about my brother, Brad. I cherished every minute, ever word I shared with my dad. Hugs were always in abundance, neither my brother nor I were ever embarrassed to hug our dad at any given time no matter how old we got or where we were. It was always difficult to have to leave him to go on a job.

NINETEEN

As was often the case, we would get the call and Scott would be on the road within a day or so headed to the next job. Sometimes I would leave with him, others I would stay behind to wrap up any business that needed handled and then I would meet him on location days or sometimes a week or so later. It was always nice to be home off a job but it was also a drain on our finances when we didn't jump from job to job. Saying goodbye to my dad was always difficult. I loved him so much. But he had a way about him, he knew that was my life, our life and he was no stranger to it. He understood, somehow that made it easier for us to say goodbye.

Scott and I had shared so many memories on the road. Life was never dull with us. We liked it that way. Since our clandestine meeting 2 years prior, Scott had moved up from being a labor hand to operating heavy equipment. Something he was not a stranger to. Since his own father owned and operated a heavy equipment business growing up. However, catching a break on the pipeline or any construction job was hard. Getting hired on as an operator meant more money and definitely a move higher up on the ladder of success.

An old boss of his called and said he had a spot for him operating at the copper mine just outside Salt Lake City. Within hours Scott was on the road and I was left behind to wrap up everything. I was going to join him in a week or so.

Before I left my dad's place on this trip he tossed something heavy towards me. Once it was in my hands I looked down to see that it was a .38 Chief revolver in a holster. Up until this point when I traveled I had our trusty dog Thor and a .44 magnum hog leg. It was so big and cumbersome that even though I kept it under the seat of my Lincoln, the sheer logistics of pulling it out to use in my defense where not in my favor. It was awkward and way too heavy for me to use effectively. Thor was a better deterrent than the hidden .44. Now that would all change, Chief has been my protector ever since.

You know how as a little kid you'd talk about what you would do to someone if they tried to hurt or kill you? For example when you watched westerns or spy shows and the subject would come up why the bad guy got killed. Well, maybe not but when I was a kid and we'd watch James Bond or John Wayne the subject would come up. On one occasion I said to my dad, "I wouldn't have killed that guy. I would have just shot him in the knees so he couldn't get away or in his crotch if he was a particularly bad guy."

From then on I learned from my father that you don't just shoot to maim you shoot to kill. We were taught to always treat a gun as if it's loaded and ready to fire. Never point it at anything you don't want to shoot and if you are in a position that your life is threatened you shoot to kill. The fact alone that your life is threatened means the attacker has the intent to kill you. That's the mindset I have had ever since then. Life is precious and valuable to me especially my own and that of people I love but if a perpetrator doesn't value his own life enough to risk it by threatening mine, than I have no regard for him either. Bert made sure to remind me that it wasn't going to be the most accurate at much past 15 feet or so but then again, if I had to shoot at that distance chances were I wasn't in a threatening situation. I was brought up shooting guns; I am a staunch supporter of the 2nd amendment. It's this simple, making me helpless doesn't make the bad guys harmless.

That day my dad gave me his .38 was a very special day in my life. This gun had served him the same way it was going to serve me. It meant a lot to me that he trusted me with it and that he knew I could handle it and handle myself. He loved me enough to make sure I could take care of myself. Even now knowing what I know about my parentage that .38 is one of my prized possessions.

TWENTY

Scott had bought me a 1977 Lincoln 2 door town car for my birthday. A beautiful car, it was in mint condition and I loved that thing. We called it the Land Barge and driving it was a dream. Mileage at that time was an issue but not a critical issue for us. The Land Barge wasn't too bad on gas considering its size and she was so comfy on road trips. Bronze in color with a rag top, it was a sharp looking car, you put that together with a little 20 year old blonde that had a cute figure and apparently that makes you a hooker in Salt Lake City, Utah.

I had left Greeley early in the morning hoping to make Salt Lake City before the end of the day. It was all new territory to me so I was excited for the adventure. Wyoming was always a drag to drive through at least the part of it on I-80 to Utah. Going through the mountains of Utah I was surprised at how absolutely majestic they were, especially around the Snow Bird Ski Resort area. This was the first time I had ever noticed the runaway truck ramps that have sand at the end of them. I quickly figured out why as to the high grades the passes where through parts of the mountains. I was just in a Lincoln and I didn't care much for the steep hills. I made my way to Salt Lake City and found the motel Scott had checked in to. We didn't have GPS then, good thing I paid attention to map reading in school.

It was late afternoon when I pulled up to the office of this motel. It was a chilly time of year so I was wearing my favorite leather coat that had a fur collar. Which apparently, is also a way that locals Identify hookers. I walked in the office and asked the guy what room Scott was in. He was rather rude and denied the fact that there was anyone there registered by that name. Did I already mention the guy was really an ass hole? I knew Scott was staying there I had just spoke with him the night before. Finally the guy relents and admits that Scott had been registered there but his bill was due that day and since he hadn't paid by 2pm he wasn't registered there now. Really, this guy was a prick. So I said that was why I was there and that I wanted to pay the bill and rent the room for a few more days. I had enough of this guy's bad attitude, so I informed him that if Scott's stuff had been messed with or removed from the room we would be having some words. The guy kept being a real jerk to me. And I couldn't figure it out I was nothing but nice to him until he started being a shit head to me. I was the customer, and you're always supposed to be nice to the customer. The guy wouldn't even let me pay the damn tab until I proved to him I was actually married to Scott. Apparently, all hookers wear gold wedding bands too, as him seeing mine wasn't proof enough I had to show him my driver's license. It was some seemingly clean looking dive motel I was trying to give my money too not the Ritz Carlton for God's sake. When I finally was able to pay the bill, get the key and go see the room I had paid for, I quickly decided I had overpaid. And if I could remember the name of the place I would have put it in this book!

It was a long drive and the recent exchange with the asshole motel owner wore me out. I shut the door behind me turned the TV on and threw myself on the bed. I looked at the wall next to me and noticed something behind a picture that was hung there. So I got up and moved the picture. I guess this guy's idea of decorating was to hang pictures over vulgarities that people wrote on the walls because under each picture on that one wall was some nasty words.

Salt Lake City didn't start off on a good note with me and it didn't get any better. Once Scott got in from work and cleaned up we went out for dinner. I didn't know that ordering anything with caffeine in it made it obvious to everyone else you were a foreigner. Great now I'm not only a hooker but have been singled out as an alien of sorts as well. The whole experience in Salt Lake City was less than stellar. From the whole hooker thing to people staring at you because they know you're an outsider once you order a Pepsi with your supper.

Standing in line at an Arby's behind a man that came in with a rather large brood ordering food that is less then healthy for you and then 15 cups of water was funny to me. It was like hey guy, you don't drink caffeine but you can eat the most sodium laced preserved food there is and that's ok? It just seemed ironic to me. Even ordering coffee with our donuts for breakfast the next morning at Donut World or whatever it was called. It seemed it was all the salesgirl could do to keep from pointing her finger at us and screeching "Outsider" so that everyone could hear.

 I stayed a couple more days before I left to return to Greeley. I didn't want to leave Scott but the job was fixing to go south anyways. The money that he was promised over the phone wasn't what he was actually getting when I got there. This happens a lot and usually ends up with us dragging up. Dragging up means leaving abruptly and sometimes not in an opportunistic moment for the employer. That would be the case on this job. The money never got settled and so Scott drug up and came home a week after me.

Since that time I've driven through Salt Lake City once in the early 90's, suffice to say I didn't stop. It's not that I hold a grudge but if I had needed gas and it was real iffy that I would make it to the nearest gas station outside of Salt Lake City. If it was imminent that I would end up walking to get some gas because I took that chance. I would still have done so. I have no desire to ever return to that town.

TWENTY ONE

Dumas Texas, we called it Dumb Ass Texas for no reason other than by looking at the spelling the similarities were striking. Dumas was the first pipeline job I worked with Scott as well as for JB McCoy and Rex Heiner. Both companies were from the Greeley area and went a long way back with each other. They had partnered up to do this job together. It was a really big job that was contracted out so that we started one end and the company that bid the other half started on other end and we met in the middle. This was a gas pipeline that was laid back when horses were used on the job. In 1987 we used Caterpillars.

Scott was breaking out as a side boom operator and I lucked out getting hired on in the field office. The whole town of Dumas was booming the time we were there only because it was wall to wall pipeliners. It seemed the bars and liquor stores where open 24 hours. Everyone had money, we worked hard and we played hard. Barbequing at nights, drinking beer and partying, swapping war stories from the day's events and regaling the jobs and antics of the past.

Pipeliner; if I had to define what one was it would be hard working hard living, adventure seeker, live on the edge and love it individual. A pipeliner is a human that was never meant to work in an office or live the mundane 9 to 5 life. Life had to be lived to the fullest or it wasn't worth it.

 For some it was the only lifestyle that accepted them. While there were pipeliners that didn't drink didn't party and didn't do drugs, I only knew a few. We were a generation of pipeliners that are about as extinct today as those types where then. During the day Scott was out on the job and I was either figuring payroll or on supply runs. Welding rods, tractor parts you name it I would spend 18 hours a day driving a company truck to Amarillo or Stinnet to get parts sometimes several runs just depended on the day.

I got pulled over one day in my Lincoln going to get the mail from the post office. I stopped at a stop sign and proceeded on. The cop that pulled me over disagreed with my stopping technique. We had been in Dumas long enough by then to have had several of our brethren, so to speak, wind up in the jail house. Lord knows no one closes a bar down better than a pipeliner so word was out that some of was were kind of rowdy. I knew the minute the lights went on behind me that I didn't do anything wrong. I also figured this guy was going to try to give me a hard time too. Sure enough, he did try; pulling me over under the guise of running a stop sign, what he really wanted was information. He questioned me about what I was doing in town. Who I worked for and that was as far as he got. The rest was none of his business and so I informed him that if he was going to give me a ticket to get on with it. But that I would contest it in court and it would be worth my while to also bring up that wasn't the only reason for him pulling me over. I wasn't acting suspicious unless you call checking the company mail every day at the post office suspicious behavior. I don't really know what his deal was but I was glad that I stood up to him once he tucked his tail between his legs and got back in his car and left me alone.

The job had been under some scrutiny regarding the fact that it wasn't a union job. We weren't a union contractor. I don't dispute the fact that at one time the unions made a big difference for the everyday Joe and workplace rights. They served a very good cause and made some huge strides and improvements. They also got big and greedy and lazy. I personally didn't care for them as much as I don't care now overall for unions. The short time Scott was a union member they didn't do a damn thing but take our money straight from his paycheck and when he needed a job they didn't do anything to help him. It was a waste of money. We found the union to be about as useful to us as boobs on a board. And trust me there were a lot of boobs. Once the job got started up the unions were sniveling about not getting this project unionized, so they had a picket line. I took great personal pleasure running that picket line every morning they were there. My point of view was if you can't see my big ole Lincoln coming down the road with the dust flying in the air, you need to be in an eye doctor's office and not on the picket line. If you're not smart enough to get out of the way as I turn into the yard than you deserve to get run over. And so for the relatively brief time I had to tolerate their pathetic little picket line I never slowed down when I turned into the yard but they did learn to scatter when they seen my Lincoln coming down the road. I loved it!

About midway through the job I had to make a quick trip to Colorado to get our trusty dog Thor. He had been under the care of a friend of ours and we missed him so I left for a couple days and went to get him. Scott got Thor before the whole explosion of how bad pit bulls were supposed to be. Like with any animal or simply any being on earth you can raise them to be violent and mean and dangerous. Pit bulls where made the poster child of dangerous breeds by irresponsible people. The truth is their breed has been abused by humans. Thor looked like a demon. Scott had got him when he was about 10 months old. When Thor got his ears cropped they left the stitches in too long so along with his demon ears they also looked kind of jagged up close. All in all you couldn't find a sweeter dispositioned dog and he loved us. We loved him. He was a bull dog and did some stupid shit but after all he was a dog. Eating my underwear the night of my senior prom and years later shitting on our bed in our fifth wheel trailer, that was just Thor. He was so much our baby that I had arranged for him to have doggie day care while we were at work because we didn't want him alone in the motel room. Every morning I got up early to take him 10 miles outside of town to a kennel and I would pick him up after work. They loved him there; he was just a big baby.

On the return run back to Texas I knew Thor had to pee. After you cross the Colorado border into the Panhandle there was this rest area of sorts. I pulled off the road and into the dirt road circling the rest area and stopped the car. I let Thor out and he took off searching for the lucky bush he was going to drown. I stretched out my legs and arms while I walked away from the Lincoln, trying to keep up and eye on Thor as he ran from bush to bush. I don't know why I looked up but I did. I saw a man behind what looked like a brick barbeque grill area and his shoulders where moving up and down. I didn't like what I saw so I casually started walking back to the car like nothing was wrong. He was as far away from me as I was from the car but if he had ran towards me I would not have had the chance to get to the car and pull the 44 out from under the seat. He started to walk a little faster than I was, at that time I considered him an imminent threat and so I called for Thor. Before I knew it here comes this demon looking bulldog out of nowhere and he runs by me and heads for the car. The creeper saw Thor and immediately stopped in his tracks and acted like he was distracted by something. Inside I breathed a sigh of relief. Thor stopped when he got to the car and waited for me to get there. The whole time I'm keeping this weirdo in my vision. Thor gets in the front seat, he always rode shot gun.

As I slide into the driver's seat trying not to turn my back or lose sight of this guy I slip my hand under the seat and bring out the 44. The door was still open and I knew he could tell that what I had just placed in my lap was a fricking big handgun. I shut the door and locked it, I was safe now. I glanced down to put the key in the ignition and when I looked up the guy was gone. I had to drive around this dirt circle drive to leave. For a split second I got scared that if I couldn't see him ahead of me he was behind me but when I pulled in there weren't any vehicles so he was on foot I quickly put as many miles as I could between me and that rest area and I never stopped there again. No matter how bad Thor or I had to pee.

Even though we all knew how dangerous pipelining could be, that was what the attraction was for many of us. The job required that you be on the top of your game. Tractors were in constant motion, trucks everywhere. The pipe was being held over the ditch by side booms. Welders were cutting out the old oxy-acetylene welds and ARC welding new pipe sections together. The job was a busy place to be and a dangerous one. Things were known to catch fire or blow up.

On the Dumas job at one time I believe we had over a 200 man payroll. Many of these men were locals who worked as labor hands. For many of them this was their first pipeline. Safety was always an issue, you can take all the steps possible in an effort to keep your guys safe but accidents happen, people get hurt and on this job one got killed.

Long story short, a labor hand leaned over the tracks of a side boom, when the operator put the tractor in gear he got sucked up under the counterweights. I knew barely enough about the labor hand to say anything and have it be accurate about his age and family. I know he had kids and that was it. Because it was a job site accident resulting in death there was an investigation and an autopsy done. When the report was issued some weeks later, a copy was sent to the field office. We had to have it on file but no one wanted it in their desk, so it ended up in mine.

My dad knew what had happened as I always called him from the road to check in. He told me to never look at the report that it would haunt me if I did. Despite my promise to follow his advice, on a rarely boring afternoon as I sat in my office I took the report out and read it. The first few pages were nothing but medical jargon regarding the forensic assessment of the man's exterior appearance. He had two legs two arms and everything was normal developmentally. The report went on to indicate where the injuries were sustained and then an accountability of all the organs and their condition, size and weight. It was all very thorough, all very clinical. I thought to myself, this is what a life comes to; a cold body on a metal table being dissected in the name of science. The man that coroner cut on was a little boy at one time. A little boy with dreams, he was someone's son, brother, husband and father and it all ended with him on that cold table.

I should have stopped there, I had no idea the following pages would be all photographs. It was too late for me to turn back once the first photograph was in view. For being sucked up under the counterweights he looked pretty good for a dead guy. Out of respect for this man I never knew I'll just leave it at that.

TWENTY TWO

It was great to be free. It was awesome to be on my own. It was beautiful to have someone I loved so much to share it all. It was because of Scott I got to experience so much and learn so much about people and places and life. Our life wasn't normal by any definition. Kids I had graduated with followed different paths some had gone straight to work others on to college. I was never the jock or the preppy, I was the loner. People knew me. More knew me than I knew of them. I stuck to a small group of friends and considered high school a necessary evil. I knew I was going to graduate there was never any other way of thinking. My life had never been normal or traditional in any sense. I was older than my years because of my childhood. And so from an early age I yearned to be free. I yearned to be anywhere than where I was at the moment. Something I still deal with frequently.

 College was a nice thought but it wasn't my dream really. I had visions of being on Wall Street, of having power and money but I didn't have visions of how I was going to get there or what the reality was to get there. The dream I prayed for ever since I knew how to pray was to have a husband and a family and to be the best wife and mother I could be. Once I found that man I was going to be loyal and the best partner I could be. So when Scott and I got together that's what I tried to do. Scott was more street wise than me in many ways. I looked up to him and I still do. I trusted him and in him. And I'm glad I did.

We were on our way to a job in Enid Oklahoma. We still had the 20ft Cobra camper at that time and were on Interstate 70 almost to Lamar Colorado. We had just caught a buzz about the time our truck caught on fire. Scott pulled over to the side of the road and popped the hood of our grey 4x4 GMC. Black smoke rolled out from under it. He had just got the flames put out when a trooper pulls up and begins to walk up the side of the vehicle. I remember Scott saying, "Don't just jump out of the truck Holly. Just stay there." I'm like yeah sure thing. Thor didn't get the same directions because as the trooper came up the back of the truck Thor jumps up. The guy goes for his sidearm but luckily realizes that Thor isn't going to hurt him. Good thing I didn't jump out of the truck too or he probably would have shot me. Honestly, I wouldn't have blamed him. How would he know if we were just a couple of kids or some maniac serial killers? I was glad I listened to Scott that day. When I eventually did get out of the truck the trooper was still a little itchy but he called us a wrecker who came and towed our truck and trailer back to a repair shop's yard. We spent that night in Lamar Colorado locked in a truck yard. Before the tow truck driver left for the night we walked over to a 7 Eleven hoping to get something good for supper, only to come back with a fine selection of convenience store junk food and some beer. We drank the beer, got stoned, ate the junk food and went to bed.

The next morning after surveying the damage to the truck it appeared all we needed was new sparkplugs and wires. I don't quite remember how the truck caught on fire but I do remember how happy I was that the repair didn't involve a whole new engine. A 75 dollar tow bill and whatever it cost for the parts and we were on the road again.

Had we any sense at that age we would have turned back then. But we forged forward and no sooner than we crossed the state line than the roll up canopy that was attached to the side of the camper tears off. I turn my head to see it hit the highway and breakup in pieces. Any hope of retrieving them vanished once the various buses, semis and cars rolled over the carnage. At that point all we could do was laugh, there was nothing else to do but laugh. We had taken a signature loan from the bank we did business with to get to this job. Our truck catches on fire almost burns to the ground, our dog almost gets shot by a trooper, we spend the night drinking beer getting stoned and eating Twinkies in a truck lot, the roll up canopy on our trailer is completely destroyed. Ohhh, and to top it off we get to Enid Oklahoma only to find out that the there was no job! Two days on the road and now we have to turn back and retrace our fated trail home and hope something comes up before we run out of pot and cash. Yup, those where the good times! Correction, that was a glimpse of all the good times.

TWENTY THREE

1988, Scott and I were on a job in Creston Iowa. Not a pipeline job, this time we were working for a contractor rebuilding a waste water treatment plant. The same one we worked for before in Bethany Missouri. It was a shitty job but somebody had to do it...that was my attempt at work place humor. Scott's dad and younger brother were also working it. I eventually got on working in the field office handling job inventory, timecards and running parts and supplies for the guys. It was good money. We still partied but not like on the pipeline, we were with a different kind of people. One thing that was similar was our sense of workplace humor and so it wasn't unheard of to send the new guy to get a pair of pipe stretchers... we knew they didn't exist but he didn't.

 Occasionally, on a job you run into that one butthead who thinks he's a genius. Engineers are supposed to be smart, or so one would think. They may be book smart but common sense seems to be the price they pay for this knowledge. You can lay out and design as much as you like but practical application will trump your design every time! My case and point... every fucked up parking lot you drive through. Anyways, we had an engineer on this job that was dumber than a bag of hammers. I don't remember if he was even a nice guy he was so stupid I didn't care to know him. The way the job was laid out the porta potty was right outside my office window. The boss couldn't take a shit without me knowing it neither could the engineer. Every morning like clockwork at around 10 a.m. this guy would take the newspaper and go visit the john for 30-45 minutes. I know because I kept track of it for the other guys who eventually took my little bit of intel and used it to plan when they were going to lock him in the poop house. The day came and the crime was done, needless to say after his bonding time on the shitter he decided he needed to look for a different job .The crew got a "talkn to" I never was implicated and we all got rid of a dumb ass. I'd say it was a win-win deal for me. I look back now, and have to stop myself from feeling bad for the guy. Here's why, he was incompetent and somewhat careless.

I liked the job boss we had. He was a good guy and a family guy. Some of the crew didn't have much respect for him but as a whole he was a decent human being. We had a supplier I would go to for welding supplies, things of that nature. The guy had taken a liking to me that made me very uneasy. On a couple of occasions he tried to look down or somehow get under my shirt. At the beginning it was all small talk. I was no stranger to construction I grew up being the boss's daughter for a construction company. Hanging with the guys and exchanging jocularities was a skill of mine. I could hold my own and even put many to shame. But this guy had gone a little far and he made me uncomfortable, so much so that after a while I would get one of the other guys to run to his shop for supplies in my place. I'd always have an excuse for why I couldn't go. Eventually my excuses ran out and I was face to face with having to do it myself. It was really hard for me to tell my boss about this guy but I just knew deep down inside that he wasn't going to give up. So I had to tell, my boss was really good about it right off the bat. He said that I never had to go there again. I really appreciated it. After all, it was my job to run supplies and parts. It wasn't until way later down the road that I found out that this guy, my boss, who I had taken a picture of leaning back in his chair asleep in the afternoon sun in his office; with the intent to bribe, blackmail or otherwise manipulate him for a good laugh, had gone after work and paid this pervert a visit to tell him to keep his paws to himself or he'd beat his ass. I still have the picture but I never did anything with it.

TWENTY FOUR

It was on this job in July that Bert passed away. My dad's death was a catastrophic loss for me. Scott and I had gone home for a few days earlier that month only to find him popping nitro pills and really not in that great of shape. He was bound and determined to finish a project he was working on before my aunts and uncles came for a dinner. The day of the dinner came and he was in worse shape. By the time my aunt got there it was all we could do to load him in her Cadillac and get him to the hospital in Denver, over fifty miles away. I had no clue what was going on. I was shocked and in disbelief that this was happening. We get to the hospital and he's in the ER for what seems like forever. Scott, my brother and I along with my aunt and uncle waited anxiously for the doctor to come out. It would be several hours before Scott, I and Brad were able to see him.

He was wired to a lot of machines that were beeping and he was on oxygen. We weren't told anything at that time about what had happened. We were just glad to see him and be with him. Before I know it he goes from talking to us to breathing harder. Alarms go off and doctors and nurses run from everywhere to where we are at. Brad and Scott make it out of the emergency room but I got cornered behind the door all I seen was a crowd of people around my dad shouting orders I didn't understand, it was all a blur of commotion. My dad was quiet and motionless I don't know how for sure I got out of the ER. I think Scott found me, grabbed me, and got me to the waiting area.

The next few days were like time stopped, I was stuck in some unbelievable nightmare. We waited for word, anything that would tell us what was happening to our dad. Tests were being done, doctors were waiting for results. This was 1988 so nothing happened quickly, then it was all hurry up and wait and hope you didn't die before you knew if there was a cure. It was very frustrating to say the least. Here was modern medicine with all the technologies of the day yet still so far back in the stone ages when it came to certain medical conditions. I found it odd that given heart transplants and all the advancements in medicine that answers were not forthcoming. I wished we had taken him anywhere but the VA Hospital.

Scott and I waited for as long as we could before we had to head back to the job in Iowa. It was an early morning; we stopped off to see my dad before we headed out. It was a 100 mile detour but one that we gladly made just so that we could see him. He wanted us to go, or at least I thought so. Looking back now I wonder if I was just that naive. I would have stayed had I thought otherwise. There was nothing I wouldn't do for my dad. We made small talk and I hugged him and kissed him I told him I loved him very much and that I would come back and help him when he got out of the hospital. When he said goodbye to Scott he knew it would be the last time he would see Bert alive. I believe my dad said something to him to the effect of, "take care of her Sport." I wouldn't know of this till years later. This was the last time I saw my dad alive.

The next week I spent on and off the phone talking with the doctors that were assigned to Bert. The damage to his heart was extensive. When it came to any prognosis I was told that he could have 2 hours, 2 days, 2 weeks 2 months or even 2 years, there was no promise and nothing was for sure. My dad knew he was sick but never said a word to me. It was his way of protecting me, I guess.

Cell phones weren't in everybody's pocket at that time. Where Scott and I had our camper parked back in Iowa there wasn't any access to phones. My aunt and I came up with a plan that if something should happen that she would call the Creston Police Department and have them come to the camper to tell me to call home.

On a sunny weekend afternoon as Scott and I sat visiting with our friends there was a knock on the door. Scott opened it to find a police officer on the steps. He was rather cranky as he was afraid of Thor and had tried to honk his car horn to get us to come to the door but we were having too much fun and didn't hear it. After the message was relayed to call home I jumped in my Lincoln and drove over to our buddies' hotel room and placed the collect call to my aunt.

"He's gone Holly"

"Oh my God, NO! How? When?"

"Just a few hours ago, I was getting ready to go up to the hospital and see him but they called first. "

I asked how my brother was doing, obviously as devastated as I was. They had to decide where to send Bert's body and so I said that the mortuary that handled our grandparent's arrangements was fine with me. After saying our "I love you's" I hung up.

Alone in a motel room over 600 miles from home, I just sat there and tried to regroup. Thinking of my dad and how scared he must have been and how he died with no family around him. I wondered why God would take my dad without at least letting somebody that loved him to be there.

I still had to go back to the camper and tell Scott. In a daze I tried to gain some composure then I left the motel and drove slowly back to relay the news, grab a few things and hit the road. When I got back to our camper Scott came out the door. He had been waiting for me. He knew in his gut already. All I could do was walk up to him and tell him that dad was gone and we needed to head home. I tried to keep walking and stay focused on the task at hand but he reached for me and held me and wouldn't let me go so we just hugged. My gut was doing flip flops, and all I could think about was locking up the camper and heading back home.

 Hours later as I'm crossing Nebraska in the middle of the night sobbing with my head in Scott's lap as he barrels down the interstate in our Lincoln trying to get to Colorado to be with Brad. I remember looking at the speedometer at 90 and telling Scott we didn't need to show up dead too.

The week we spent making the arrangements and dealing with legalities was all surreal. Discussing what our father might like best as we casket shopped in the mortuaries showcase room. What we were going to bury our dad in and how everyone was going to be told so that they could come pay their respects.

Bert was a simple man. He lived a simple life. He didn't have a closet full of suits, he didn't need them. Scott and I bought a nice dress shirt for him to wear under his suit jacket he wore when we got married and along with his dress pants, underwear and a pair of socks that's what we buried him in. No need for his special made boots that zipped up the side or for his cane and crutch. He wouldn't need them anymore.

I was already unhappy with the mortuary, they had continuously bugged my brother the whole time about arrangements while I was on the road doing the best I could to get their quickly. Brad kept telling them nothing would be decided until Scott and I got there. I thought this was extremely inappropriate and was totally driven by money. Here were two kids dealing with the sudden loss of the primary figure in their life, now having to make decisions and grieve at the same time. Our father had left a life insurance policy that would cover the expenses.   It just irked me.

When it came time to view my father I didn't know if I could do it. I dragged my feet till the last minute. When Scott and I finally went it was almost an hour before they closed for the day. I asked Scott to go in and be sure that no one was with Bert. I wanted to be alone with my dad. The minute I got to the doorway and I seen the casket and I saw the lifeless shell laying in it the first thing I thought was that wasn't my dad. My dad didn't look like that. He didn't have his glasses on and that just wasn't my dad. I walked up to his casket and I touched his hand. I could still see the bruises from IV's and such despite the mortuary putty they tried to cover it up with. His hand was cold and hard. I was too afraid to touch anything else. All I could do was just sit in a chair. Nothing was processing in my mind I was just numb. I couldn't really cry, what good would that do? My dad was always bigger than life to me. That shell I was staring at now was once animated by his perseverance, determination, positive spirit and goodness. That shell was a ball and chain to him for the last 25 years or so of his life. Those arms and huge hands gave me the best hugs that I was never going to feel again. No one was going to sing Johnny Cash Songs to me anymore. I was never going to hear my father call me "Babe" again. That sweet endearing nickname only my dad called me. It made me feel extra special. It made me feel so very loved. The biggest thing above all else I had lost my beacon. That shining light I used to navigate through life.

I too, was then no more. While I still breathed I was nothing more than flotsam floating in dead space. I was kicking and screaming on the inside, lost, scared, weeping and sobbing. On the outside I never let on. I felt I had to be strong for my brother; I had to be strong because I was still left behind. The death of my father was final. There was no argument that would bring him back. I only had one choice and that was to keep moving forward.

My life had a somber tone to it. We returned to Iowa and back on the job in Creston. The company was so sweet to have sent me a beautiful flower bouquet I only wished I felt as cheery as the flowers looked. All I could do was keep on moving on. I was constantly being faced with my loss by every well wisher that came to see me in my office.

TWENTY FIVE

We finished that job later in the fall and with the little bit of money left over from my dad's insurance we decided to settle down and buy a house. I had quit taking birth control pills once my dad got sick hoping that he would live long enough to see his first grandchild.

 The holidays rolled around and we found a place that was cheap and had promise, a real fixer upper. January, 1989, we were the proud owners of 5 acres of land and a big old house. Two kids and a bulldog out in the country with no clue whatsoever what we just got into. We threw all our money into the place and used some credit cards as well. It still wasn't enough money and soon we were broke and with no income. Scott started hauling grain and commodities for a local farmer.

Being a truck driver meant being away from home but that didn't keep me from getting pregnant. I knew almost immediately that I was expecting. My body changes where obvious. I quit smoking cigarettes cold turkey and of course did the same with the booze and dope. I wasn't what you would call an addict or junkie I just liked to party. I didn't need these things to live my life they just made the party better. What did bother me and what did bring on the beginning of marital tensions was that Scott wasn't pregnant and he didn't stop any of it. This was a way of life for him and when he was on the road the smoking and speed was how he functioned. While I was dealing with pregnancy issues and all the insecurities that come with a first pregnancy he was dealing with the anxiety of being a dad and raising a child. While I was trying to make ends meet, Scott was doing drugs to run harder and faster to make enough money to cover his habit and still give me what I needed for bills. It was a viscous chain of dependency.

With my father gone I was down to just my mother. The relationship never being a consistently stable one, it was all I had left. We had been getting along in the past months since my dad's death. We were actually getting along before that too. The 600 or so miles that separated us served as a great buffer and so between the occasional phone call and card we had been getting along. The fact that I was now pregnant made us even closer. At this point despite all the ugliness we were family and families stick together through thick and thin. There had been such caverns of hurt and anger in the past but for the time being she was being the mother that I needed and I was grateful for it. So I let my guard down hoping it would last.

The life Scott and I had didn't get any easier. The lying about where the money was going to and the fact that he was with his friends when I needed him with me wasn't any help. So I prayed. I prayed and I prayed and I prayed all the time every day. I loved my husband so very much I just wanted him to be better.

 When I got further along the months got colder, our baby wasn't due till January third. The November of 1989 was a bitter cold one. Temperatures plummeted and without any money for propane and already owing the propane company we were without heat. We used what little credit we had on a credit card to buy two kerosene heaters but even they were costly to operate and only heated the front room and kitchen of our huge old house. So I went into stay with Scott's mom when it was too cold to be home.

December came and the weather didn't show any signs of mercy. Even though I had ridden with Scott off and on for the last 8 months I was way too pregnant and required too many pit stops to pee to be able to ride anymore with him. So by mid-December I just stayed with Scott's mom full time.

In the wee hours of December 20th, I went into labor. No one was up yet the house was quiet it was about 3 a.m. My water hadn't broke yet but I was having contractions. It was a beautiful time for me when everything else in my life was spiraling out of my control. Just me and my baby, I'd wait for a contraction and time it and then wait again. In between contractions I tried to keep the excitement of finally being able to hold my baby and being a mommy, to a minimum.

Several hours later my contractions were still steady and progressing. My mother in law headed into work to wrap up a few things, thinking we still had some time left. I wasn't so sure myself. In the meantime me and my little brother in law, who was 11 or so at the time, stayed at home and timed the contractions.

It was arctic cold outside; I hadn't started my Lincoln in days. I went out to see if it would start in case we needed to head to the hospital but it was froze solid. We were stuck. Finally, about 10a.m. or so Joyce came and got us and we headed to the hospital. Calls had already been sent out to try and catch Scott where he was getting unloaded at next. Our baby was early. We figured we still had three weeks or so left. Scott was on his way to Carlsbad New Mexico to load some pot ash. There was no way he was going to make it back to see his first child born.

Lying there in the birthing room going through the contractions and squeezing my mother in laws hand so tightly I almost broke it, Zachary Dylan Cronk was born December 20th 1989. He was a tiny thing just over 6 pounds and premature but otherwise healthy and hungry. Scott heard the sound of his first son cry over the phone as he was waiting to get loaded in New Mexico. It would be another 30 hours before he would hold his son for the first time.

I was discharged the following morning and returned to stay with my mother in law. That afternoon when Scott got in I Watched him pick up and cradle our little boy in his arms for the first time. It is a moment I will always remember. I was 22 years old, Scott was 24. It was this memory and the many before that I held dear to my heart, retaining them as strength to keep me on the path that I thought was best for my family.

Things didn't get any better between us or financially after Zac was born. We still had love, just no money. If it weren't for the charge accounts we had at the local truck stop and Wilson's Grocery in Hopkins we wouldn't have had food on the table or fuel for me to go to work. Every paycheck I had was gone before I got it. After paying the babysitter, buying diapers, paying our charge accounts and then the monthly bills, we had less than nothing left. Scott was busy doing everything but being there for me while I felt abandoned and locked into a situation I couldn't improve. In no way was I going to call it quits yet something had to be done.

 My mother and sister had come to stay after Zac was born. The visit hadn't gone well. Our old house wasn't to her liking and neither was our life and she no doubt knew Scott was being a butt head at the time. All these factors and her own emotions fed into one big shit storm and erupted. We ended up arguing and it ended with her leaving.

As my life continued down the gutter at warp speed we had to let our car be repossessed and borrow a vehicle from Scott's parents. I did have a job at this time working for a doctor in town but I couldn't make enough to keep us above board. So after an argument with Scott I called my mother to come and get us. It was a huge mistake and I lived to regret it. I would be wrong to not give her credit for driving all night nonstop and spending money she didn't have to get to Missouri to pick up Zac and I. But once we got back to her place in Colorado it didn't take long before she flipped out.

Usually this would happen because we weren't doing what she expected us to do or behaving how she expected us to behave. It was always about her expectations and versions of what was right and wrong. Even when she threw around the word unconditional she didn't mean it in the way Webster's dictionary did. It was impossible to know what it was she expected of us so we lived on the edge of our nerves around her.

I let my guard down this time. I needed my mother. She tried to help I have no doubt but then her unrealistic expectations got in the way and Zac and I had to leave. Scott's sister lived in Greeley at that time and so she got us and brought us back to Maryville. I never felt more stuck in my life. There was no where I could go, I got reeled in back to Missouri, back to Scott nothing was going to change; I was scared this was the best I could ever hope for.

The weekend I got back there was a family dinner at Scott's parents. It would be the first time I was going to see Scott since I left him almost two weeks earlier. I remember standing on the front porch telling him I was back because I had no choice and that was all it was. Inside I was so heartbroken. I loved this man so much and knew he could be so much more ... he could be better; I knew this because the last 5 years together I witnessed it. I just wanted my best friend and partner back again.

TWENTY SIX

I returned to work and life returned to its fucked up normalcy. The short respite that Scott had from the drugs was just a dream and life went on. Zac was 6 months old when I realized I was pregnant again. I was in no physical shape to have another baby let alone marital or financially. Scott and I obviously were getting along on some level or I wouldn't have gotten knocked up. Despite all our differences I still lived for him. I still clung on our time before we bought the house, before the babies. I knew what we had been to each other and what we could still be. I just couldn't figure out how to show Scott that. Nothing I tried worked and most always ended up in heated arguments.

Scott was in too deep with his fast friends and fast life. I had actually decided that I had to take steps to insure that Zac and I would be taken care of I knew I couldn't do it alone but the thought of being with any other man besides Scott was something I didn't entertain for long. I just couldn't do it. So I prayed.

I can't speak for my husband but I know the man. Addiction never goes away. You can stop being a junkie but you will always be an addict. Addicts have a need for some release in their life. Cigarettes, pot, speed, booze. It covers pain and hurt, it helps sooth stress and nerves. It's a nasty parasite, a plaque among men that steals your soul and spirit. Your perceptions are dulled and your judgment is completely gone.

During the time I was pregnant with our second child nothing got better. Things would level out for a short time and then plummet. Never regaining what was lost. I hung on every word Scott said. Promises about how much his check would be and how much I would have for bills. Promises about time spent at home that really ended up just being him asleep on the couch. I counted on him to hold up to what he would tell me. It was the reason for all our arguments at that time. I was just foundering barely making things work to keep a roof over our heads and food on the table. The house was falling down around us and so was our life. Dealing with one baby and another on the way and a husband that was unreliable, keeping the wolves off our door step was all I could do. Our arguments began to get physical. I was just as much to blame. I was hurting so much. I hurt so deeply to the core, I felt betrayed and lied to. Here was the man I loved. The love of my life and I doubted he felt the same about me. But I was in this now, myself, too deep. I just knew we could see our way through if I just held on. So I prayed. I experienced a hurt that had no bounds. I wanted him to know that. My words meant nothing to him so a slap or a punch turned into a scuffle. At that time it never went past a push or shove type exchange.

TWENTY SEVEN

I was 6 months pregnant with our baby, and I was already bigger than the door was wide. I spent my last trimester praying our baby would come early. Jacob Wyatt Cronk waited to almost the very day I was due. On March 21, 1991 our second son was born. This time Scott was there to hold his son. Jake was a healthy 8 pounder baby. Dad was sick and run down and never looked worse in his life.

Now we were three and still normalcy for us was everyone else's fucked up. Through the last few years there had been some short periods of bliss. Scott would lay off the crap things would go ok. Id maybe even get a little hopeful and then the wagon would tip over and so would my dreams and hopes. I clung to these times. Communication was not our strong suit during the past years. I couldn't find a way to get Scott to understand where I was coming from. And to him I was a manipulative, nagging wife. Every time we would have an argument he would conveniently have to leave in the truck and have no time to talk about it.   Every time our arguments where over finances and his partying. With two babies at home I could not just leave and be gone for hours or an evening to hang out with friends. One of us had to stay home. I couldn't just do anything I liked without regard for anyone. I had two babies at home that needed me. Scott didn't seem to get this nor did he seem to care and that hurt.

Our finances had become something comparable to the mess we call our national deficit by early 1992. We were in over our heads and I was in over my financial skill level. Looking for help that really wasn't there I fell into the creditor relief craze. For a small deposit or fee they would help you deal with your creditors and negotiate a smaller payment. Our payment was still cumbersome and the fee just added to our debt.

  Scott knew we weren't getting anywhere with him driving truck, something had to change. So he applied to and was hired by a big company that constructed big electric towers and such. It was a sweet gig but meant that if you wanted to stay with them you had to travel. We were fixing to lose our house anyways and had nothing else to lose. The boys weren't old enough for school yet so we decided to do it. When the job was done in Maryville, Scott and his buddy headed to California to work for the same company.

The plan was that the boys and I would temporarily wait in Missouri until we had the money to meet up with Scott again. Every week he sent money home, a lot of money. Enough money to make me hopeful again those good things were around the corner. After celebrating Jakes one year birthday, an overweight out of shape momma of two of the sweetest baby boys ever, boarded a jet plane headed for Reno Nevada.

I will never forget the looks of shock and awe from the other passengers as the three of us boarded the plane. I don't know what they were thinking. Not sure I want to. I strapped a 2 ½ year old Zac in the seat next to me, and held Jacob on my lap. As the plane shimmied and shook down the runway and blasted off Zac held on the side arms of his seat and with big wide eyes all I heard him say was, "ohhhhhhhhhhh shhiiiiittttttt!"

 I was really excited for the whole trip and time in California I viewed it as an adventure. We stayed at Circus Circus in Nevada. I thought the kids, even though they were little would still like it. I hadn't seen Scott for a couple months and I was hoping to have my husband back.

 He had to rent a car to come get us; Reno was just a few hours away from Redding California where the job was. He met up with us that evening. I knew instantly when I seen him things weren't right. I felt like an alien being in his life. I felt worthless. I was overweight, wore out and really just as lost as he was but doing the best I could to keep moving forward and hoping for a better day and praying.

TWENTY EIGHT

We left Reno the next day and drove on to Redding California. It was a quiet ride. I felt like an intruder. We rented a kitchenette at the Monterey Motel. It had a pool for the kids and was close to shopping which was good since we didn't have a car. There were other guys there that worked with Scott and they had vehicles. It was a clean motel and decent priced. The pool was kept up and it had air conditioning and cable TV. Settling in was easier than feeling like my presence was wanted.

I stocked the kitchen and made sure food was on the table when Scott got home. The boys and I spent the days by the pool or inside watching TV and playing. One of Scott's friends had a convertible Cadillac he would let me borrow to go shopping or take day trips in. so I would load the boys up and we would take off on an adventure. We went to Whiskey Lake and some other local sights. Life became kind of ordinary. I had made a few friends and we spent time together. I was long done nursing the boys so I was able to party a little, always careful about it but really how does careful equate into getting stoned or snorting a line of crank. It's my biggest shame that I even did it at all. I just did it to do it. I didn't need it. It did help me get along better with Scott.

As a parent I consider any and all recreational drug use throughout my parenting life as a gigantic black eye on my character. All children, especially mine, deserve better. Children deserve parents who are "present".

My view on smoking pot outside of raising kids is different. With the current movement to legalize marijuana there is a lot to consider and requires an open and unbiased mind. I come from a generation or culture of drug abusers. We clearly did not have the scientific or medicinal benefits of pot in mind when we used it. Acting irresponsibly with this drug gave it a bad reputation, one that it did not deserve. For man to vilify a drug because its powers were misused is wrong. We are an over medicated society, over medicated by chemical compounds designed in a lab by scientists. Sure many of these chemical compounds have an organic origin; however, if I were in pain and was given the choice of taking a designer drug or smoking a joint, I would take the pot hands down. Pot is grown by Mother Nature and is an effective pain killer on its own, untouched by man's intervention or manipulation in its original form. Even though I don't smoke pot now nor have I in over 11 years, I don't know what the future holds in that regard in my private life. However, I do hope that the countless uses of marijuana and its derivatives continue to be explored and applied in everyday life from herbal and dietary supplements to even clothing and other uses. Who knows maybe someday my awesome talent of making a pipe out of aluminum foil will end up making me millions.

The noose with drug testing was starting to get tighter and tighter. Stress over knowing that alone brought troubles to my life again. My brother sold my dad's old place and so I had some money in the bank. Scott found a Bronco II that was a decent price and in great shape so we bought it. I still had money left over and we put it in a savings account. We still had creditors on our doorstep but I knew that we were facing bankruptcy and so they could keep barking all they wanted.

Now I could take day trips anywhere I wanted. The boys and I went everywhere. Lassen Volcano, Shasta Lake, rode the elephants at the Shasta County Fair. Anywhere I wanted to go we did.

On one weekend I planned a trip for us all to take to the coast and see the Redwoods. I was so looking forward to it. Scott was on edge the whole time and it made us all uncomfortable. It was tense and it made what I had hoped would have been a really nice trip, one that I just wished I forgot about.

For the first time in California I saw people begging on the street corners, dirty and holding signs. Initially they kind of scared me I had never seen anything like that before. Then it was just sad. It made me sad for them and made me glad for what I had.

In the motel there was a woman with kids staying there. A church had put her up there to help her out. They had nothing of their own. When we would barbeque on the grill if the coals were still hot she would come and ask if she could use them to cook her kids some hot dogs. We always obliged and even would give her food and stuff for her kids. It made my life and the predicament I was in privately seem so trivial compared to hers. The glass was half full for me but it was half empty for her.

The shit hit the fan when the company Scott was working for waited till all the guys were in the yard, before they headed to the jobsite, to tell them they all needed to take the 'whiz quiz' right then and there. No time to get clean pee no choice but to take the damn thing and hope you get something lined out on another job before the results come back and you get fired.

Scott came home that night with the news. Yes, he was going to test positive. We had about three days before they cut all of the flunkers loose and so he had a line on a job in Tracy California. Once they fired him, he was headed to Tracy and I would follow later. The whole deal made me uneasy. It was one thing for me to stay behind in Missouri, that was home territory, but quite another to stay behind in Redding. I couldn't take the chance of running out of money and never getting home if I needed to. But I agreed I would wait a few days and then head that way, giving him time to get a motel lined out.

TWENTY NINE

Tracy was a shithole, everything about that town including the smell from the tomato factory or whatever it was, stunk. Scott had rented a room at a Hotel Eight in a less seedy part of town. The boys and I did follow him there but I knew the minute I got in the room that this wasn't going to work. That happy vibe just wasn't there. Once more I was unsure about the work scenario and the money. Scott was less than forthcoming with the information I needed to handle the business that needed to be handled. He just didn't know or didn't ask. It was like I wasn't wanted there. He didn't want me and the boys there I could tell, for whatever reasons. I could also understand though at the same time. I didn't want the boys there either. He knew it wasn't the life we wanted for them. Yet he couldn't change things at that moment.

Our mouths started running overtime and the end result was after a day in Tracy California the boys and I were loaded up in the truck headed back to Redding California to close the bank account and head west. I didn't know if I would see Scott again. My job was to protect our babies no matter how hard it would be for me personally it was all about our boys. Everything else was secondary. Despite our differences I knew Scott felt the same way. It was all about those babies, he may not be able to have helped himself at that time but he knew he didn't want that for his sons. I gave Scott time to say good bye to the boys and without a word said between us and just tears in my eyes we left.

It was already early evening when we left Tracy. The boys had slept most of the way to Redding. I cried every mile of it. Franticly trying to figure out what my next steps were. By the time I got to Redding it was almost midnight. I had the money so we stayed at a really nice little motel. I carried Zac then Jake into the room and tucked them in bed. Locking the bronco then the door to our room I slid in between my little guys and cried myself to sleep.

The sun peeked in between the curtains the bright warmth on my face gently nudged me to consciousness. The kids needed baths and some playtime. I didn't have to check out for another 3, 4 hours so that's what we did. I eventually called my mother in law to tell her I was going to be headed her way at some point. Scott had already called her and told her I left him. He was worried about us I assured her I was ok and that I'd be seeing her in a few days. She could tell Scott whatever she wanted to. I had other things to worry about. After the boys where bathed and dressed, ready for the day, they played and watched cartoons while I made arrangements at the bank to go in and close my account out. I repacked for the long day's journey, loaded the kids and we were off. I had several thousand dollars left in the account which was great, that was enough insurance for me to feel comfortable with driving across to get to Colorado then Missouri. Once our business was handled and I got some breakfast for the kids we started on our long trek home.

THIRTY

Both Zac and Jake traveled well. Even as babies when Scott and I would take them in the truck they always did great. It made the drive time easier for me as they napped and sipped on their sippy cups. When I stopped to pee they both got changed as well.   My face was so swollen from crying the past couple of days so it didn't matter that all I did was cry as they slept and I drove.

 I thought driving across Kansas and Wyoming sucked terribly until I drove across Nevada. We made it to Elkhart Nevada before I had to call it a night. I phoned my mother in law again to check in and let her know where we were. I had decided earlier that day that I was going to drop in and visit my mother and sister before I headed to Missouri.

The day's drive had helped me get regrouped and come up with some kind of plan. With all the demons that plagued my husband I knew one thing for certain; he would see to it that his boys were taken care of. Granted it wasn't the best he could do but he never stopped trying. I knew he never would. I don't know why I just knew this. I figured I would stay a couple days with my mom and then head to Missouri and stay with Joyce, my mother in law, until I found a place in town.

The next morning we were up, got breakfast, and hit the road. I didn't stop driving until I pulled up in front of my mom's place in Greeley Colorado. She was surprised to see me but happy, real happy to have time with her grandsons. For all she knew

Scott and I agreed that raising the boys in California wasn't what we wanted for them so I headed home.

We had a nice visit but I was ready to carry on and forge forward. Missouri meant back to the same culture and friends that incubated my husband's addictions but it also meant I had family around me and it was a small town I wasn't going to get lost anywhere.

It was good to be back in Maryville and I was even more relieved to have found a cute little house in town for the right price. So I used up the money I had left to put a down payment and first month's rent on it. Scott and I had established an agreement regarding the finances and so I had money coming in. I spent the day's taking care of our sons and just living.

I answered an ad to do appliqué work for a local business. I could work at home and still make money so it was the perfect opportunity for me. The boys started preschool a couple days a week. I tried real hard to make things normal and to offer them the best environment I could. Plenty of Legos, plenty of Disney, lots of play and learning time and endless love and cuddles.

A few months passed and Scott wanted to come home. I don't remember if the job was done or what exactly, it really didn't matter he was coming home all the same. Arrangements were made for him to fly home. The boys and I picked him up from the airport. He looked good but I knew things hadn't changed. I just felt it. His body language was all off. As usual there would be a bliss period like when you get a new puppy. Scott went back to trucking but for a better company and his attempts to stay away from the wrong crowed were valiant yet still failed. We were back on the relationship roller coaster and I was getting worn thin. The boys were getting old enough that I didn't know what they would and wouldn't remember. I didn't want them to know their mommy and daddy couldn't get their shit together. I didn't want them to think their mommy was weak so she kept them exposed to a terrible lifestyle because of it. There had to be something better out there in the world …

THIRTY ONE

It always seems to come down to promises made that were unkempt. I needed to be able to trust in his word. I paid the bills and handled the finances he was the main family income. More often than not the two never reconciled. The hammer of doom was always hanging close above. Upon returning to Missouri I did file for bankruptcy, unfortunately the lies didn't go away with the creditors. I tried so very hard to talk to Scott to try and get him to understand but it was like talking to a wall, an unforgiving brick wall. Nothing I said ever made a difference. I was the bitch at the house, the ball and chain. All I wanted was to be able to rely on my husband and to know he was good to his word. I couldn't do my job if he wasn't doing his. The amount of stress in my life was tremendous. It didn't just appear out of nowhere it began to build up when we had Zac. I got my first ulcer in 1991 things just went downhill after that. Now it's early 1993 and I couldn't have felt more worthless in my life than I did then.

I don't remember how these people came into my life but I began donating to a church thru the mail. I think it started with me sending away for something for the boys, most likely bible stories. I remember sending donations and the pastor sent me my first devotional, I still have it to this day. We exchanged letters and I was grateful for the interaction we shared. To have that connection that someone cared meant a lot to me. God never left me but I was beginning to wonder just how strong he thought I was.

I had hopes that my sewing side job would grow into something bigger. I wanted to be able to not have to rely on Scott. I could easily see making Zig-Zag unlimited a profitable appliqué and machine embroidery business. But it just wasn't meant to be.

One evening Scott came home and was there long enough to tell me he was leaving to do something else. He had just got in from driving truck and then he was leaving with a buddy. I couldn't take it anymore. I really didn't feel I had anything to lose. I sure didn't feel loved by any means and my self-worth couldn't have been any lower. My heart was beyond broken I just couldn't understand how things could go so terribly awful for us when we meant so much to each other for those years before we had kids. I just wanted to understand how and why. I was hurt, so very hurt and all I had were words so we argued. The argument escalated I reached out for Scott hoping I could look in his eyes and make a connection somehow. Now it was physical. My head met the kitchen cabinet drawers a few times. I was mad as hell then. Never backing down can be a great characteristic, not when it comes to physical aggression. But that's how I am. I knew I was going to get hurt, I also knew I was going to do my fair share of damage along the way. It was a quick tiff and he was out the door. His buddy was still waiting for him in his car by the curb. I knew then I had to do something for my boys. I knew the life we had since Scott came back to Missouri was not going to be any better and we had no chance to break the cycle.

I loaded my babies in the truck and we went to the police station. I filed a report, let them take some pictures of my face and neck and then we went home and locked the doors. It was late evening by the time we got home I got the boys ready for bed and I laid between them as we all drifted to sleep. Around midnight there was a knocking on the front door.

I was startled, not knowing who it could be. Peeking through the curtains I seen it was a policemen so I answered the door. He had come to let me know that Scott had been bailed out of jail by his mother. That was great news, I wondered how pissed he was. I knew no matter what he felt at that point that it was of no concern to me nor would it ever be anywhere close to the blackest depths of heartache I had been living with.

The next morning Scott's mom, called to see if they could come get the boys for the day. I woke up really stiff and sore and had a killer headache. I knew Scott would never hurt our babies .Our kids were always our common ground, besides his mom would be with them. I wasn't going to be very good for them until I got healed up so I agreed. I got the boys ready and grandma came to get them. There I was in this little white house all by myself. I was so sore all I could do was lie prone on the bed and cry. I had no idea what to do next; I was lost, alone and devastated knowing how my life was turning out was not how I ever imagined.

The boys ended up staying the night at their grandma's house with Scott. I had spent that whole day in bed and I really should have tried to walk around but I couldn't move. Physically, emotionally and mentally I was completely drained. I missed my babies but I was no good to them this way. I spent that night crying and praying.

The sun came up and it was mid-morning. Scott was coming through the front door with our babies. I was still lying in bed. Within seconds he was standing in the doorway of our bedroom. We made small talk. That's all it was, not one word of it had any meaning, dead words like the dead space that separated us. I so wanted some acknowledgement that maybe things would be better but none came. He asked if I wanted him to take the boys for another day. I wasn't going to have any of that. I forced myself off the bed and out into the living room. Nothing put a bigger prouder smile on my face than those two little boys of ours. Just seeing them made me feel a little better. Despite what a shitty life I had to offer them hopefully they were still too young to know what was going on in their world. For that much I thanked God. Scott left and so for the next few days I tried to pick up and move on. It was just the three of us. It really had been all this time to begin with.

I decided I was going to take them to Colorado for a visit to see my mother and sister. After I rounded up enough money I packed our bags and we headed west. I had no idea when I left Maryville that morning it would be 10 years before I'd move back.

THIRTY TWO

My big brother had sent me a hundred bucks to get the things we needed and to make the trip with. There weren't any signs left on my body that would tattle tale on me about how physical our fight had been and I don't believe I ever brought up that aspect to my family.

Once we got to Colorado my mother was so happy to see her grandsons nothing else mattered. I was lost and really just couldn't get my bearings I just tried to decompress. On the way out my Bronco kept heating up and then cooling back down. I thought it was a stuck thermometer. So we had a mechanic my mom knew take a look at it. It turned out I was pretty lucky to have made it across as the radiator needed replaced as well as some hoses. The work would take a couple of days and meant that my trip home would be delayed. The timing of it lent itself well to what took place while the truck was in the shop. I like to think it was God stepping in. I got a call that Scott hadn't taken our absence very well and had gotten into trouble. At that point I felt I had no choice but to consider options outside of the box. I knew going back condemned me to more of the same. But I was scared. I didn't want to fuck things up worse than they were. I really needed my mother, and this time she was there for me.

The hardest part about dealing with my mother is that it is beyond difficult for me to understand how someone who gave birth to me, loved me and raised me could also be mean, hateful and unpredictable. What she did for me during the next few months was a lifesaver. She offered me a lifeboat and I took it. They boys and I were going to stay in Colorado and start a new life. I had to put them first and nothing else mattered. I knew this was the right decision. It also opened a door to uncharted territory. I placed the call to Missouri and asked my mother in law to pack up our house that I wasn't coming back and to tell Scott that I was staying in Colorado.

Together my mother, little sister and I built a life around the boys. I got my certification to flag on construction jobs and spent that whole summer working on jobs all over Weld and Larimer County. One of the prettiest jobs I was on was a resurfacing job on the roads that lead up to and around Horsetooth Reservoir. I loved watching the sun come over the mountains and shine down on the lake surface. I would watch the boats and skiers zip by. Wishing I was with them and remembering all the times I would go camping at that same lake with the Hilzer's. Spending the day swimming and riding in my uncle's boat.

It's nasty work following a paver. The heat they put out laying asphalt can make an already miserably hot day 10 times worse. Eventually, I took a job with a concrete company driving a truck and setting up traffic and road signs for the chip seal crew. We worked 6 sometimes 7 days, 12-18 hours depending on where we were at. It was hard work but I made great money.

While I was at work my mom and sister teamed up to watch the boys. When my mother had to work Mandy watched them. It was a blessing that we all got along. I think it was because my mom loved having her grandsons close to her and she felt good about helping me. I was grateful for her being there. On my days off we would go to the mountains or the Denver Zoo. We always tried to do things with the boys.

Joyce and Scott packed up the house and sent me some things that we needed, the rest went into storage. Scott was staying with his mom and seemed to be getting himself back together again. We chatted occasionally and exchanged letters. It was clear that I had no intention of moving back to Missouri. If he wanted to be a part of our lives again he had to prove it. So he did.

I was skeptical, despite that I wasn't ready to divorce him. I couldn't do that. I didn't feel that I had tried hard enough to be able to walk away with a clear conscience. I wanted more for my boys. I remembered the man I married even if he didn't. I didn't understand why he did the stupid things he did, neither did he. I knew how hard my mother struggled to be a single parent of three. I didn't want that. Throughout everything our kids have always been the center. Even if Scott and I didn't see eye to eye or weren't getting along he was still there for birthdays and family events. We always came together for our children. I knew he would always see that his kids were taken care of. As for me I just felt like the baggage that came with the kids. When I needed him he was nowhere to be found. I felt I could live with this as long as the kids were raised by both mom and dad. I couldn't give them a better life if I couldn't be there for them because I had to work some shitty job all the time.

They never heard a negative word from me about their dad, ever. Every card was from the both of us with lots of love. Every present was the same. No matter how bad things were between us, I always kept their dad in the picture, even when he was gone he was still present just by how I talked to the boys.

It was late summer in 1993, jobs were slowing down. Scott had cleaned up and was sounding like the man I loved. The man I needed. So I made a quick trip back to Maryville to get him and bring him to Colorado.

THIRTY THREE

I hadn't seen Scott in months, I almost didn't recognize him, and he looked good. I had my hair cut short and was tanned from working outside. I was still overweight but not as much as when I left Missouri. When we saw each other it was a joyful reunion but I had rode this horse before and been bucked off. He was going to have to really work for me to get over being skeptical.

On the return trip we got all caught up and talked about making a new life in Colorado. And about the fact that he had some proving to do and that we had some work to do. We were such great partners and best friends when we started out. It was us against the world and we conquered it. Where we made the wrong turn I'm really not sure. To place blame on only Scott would be unfair. It is true he battled addiction and dependency but I was so wanting his approval that I was codependent to a degree, I was floundering in the world without my pillar of positivity, my father, and still reeling back and forth with the on and off relationship with my mom. All of this and more was the perfect mix for failure.

Days after Scott and I returned we agreed to share a house with my mom and sister. My mother had found the perfect place next to a park. We would rent the basement and she would live on the ground floor. Finding a decent place at that time in Greeley was hard. This seemed to be a great idea. Scott got on with an oilrig company and was working long hours 6 days a week, money was coming in. The economy was different in Colorado than Missouri so going from that economic climate to this one was a plus. Things were booming again in Weld County, it was a good time to come back to my home state and old turf.

Our bliss of cohabitating was short lived as my mother was on edge with Scott's presence. She wasn't seemingly happy about the fact that when he was home he was resting. When a guy works 6 days a week 18 hour days I'd say on the 7th day he needs to rest. But she didn't see it that way. In all honestly, she never really thought very highly of men in general. That's the impression I got. I don't think Scott could have done anything right in her eyes no matter what. It was obvious to me that any preconceived notion she had that was probably farfetched to begin with was not materializing. The environment became stressful and I could feel the tension in the air. It was like being a kid again and just wondering what it was that was going to cause her to blow. And blow it did.

Scott and I had gone to wash his work clothes at the laundry mat and when we came back things just blew up. We were gone 2 ½ hours doing laundry, she thought that was too long and that's all it took for words to fly. My mother has a venomous tongue. It's really no use trying to explain yourself to her or try to gain her understanding because it never happens. Everyone but her has a twisted perception of reality, there is only one way to be or to view things and that's her way. You're all wrong in every other way. As far as she is concerned it's an illness that requires those who contradict or challenge her to seek help. She never admits to being wrong. She is, however, very sad for those who don't agree with her because the twisted world they live in is unhealthy.

You can't argue with that it just maxes out your frustration levels. When she can accomplish this then things can get physical. My mother has been known to raise a hand to me to try and slap me. When I was a teen and old enough to finally do something I blocked her move. She had bad mouthed my father I stood up to her she tried to slap me and I blocked it. The next morning real early before school I loaded my car with all my clothes and things I would need and never came back. I was just barely 16 then. This time when she started to slap me I blocked her again and then I put her in the corner. I easily had 75 pounds on her. She has a knack for verbally backing people in a corner you may not physically be anywhere near one but you'd still feel it. This time after her failed attempt that's where she ended up. She could never shut her mouth. The mean hateful things she said. Things I could and never would think of saying or calling my child.

During the argument Scott got the boys and loaded them in the Bronco he came back to get me and had to grab me from behind. She was still spewing her hate and I was dumb enough to stick around and bandy words with her. Her parting words were to call me a fat bitch. True or not it still hurt coming from my own mother.

THIRTY FOUR

There we were, a Bronco II with the four of us and nowhere to go. We couldn't go back to the house. We were very fortunate that Scott's sister lived in Greeley and could put us up for a few days. Scott went to work and I tried to find us a new place to live. Finding anything was difficult at that time. With the gas fields booming again in Weld County rentals were scarce.

I was really worried about finding a place. Our friend who lived close by was going to be leaving on a pipeline job and it worked out that we would rent his house and keep it maintained. We'd do some fixer up projects in exchange for a break in the rent. The neighborhood wasn't the best. In fact it was the unincorporated part of Evans Colorado. The sheriff's office called it the Jungle. But it wasn't all that bad, things could have been worse and it was a house. So we took it.

It was about October of 1993 the house we had been fortunate enough to take over needed a lot of TLC. I had plenty of time during the days, while the boys played, to clean and organize and try to make it a home. After the rampage at the previous house I hadn't had much contact with my mother for a while. It didn't last long it was nothing new just part of the cycle of our relationship. Eventually, we began to talk again and she was once again in our lives. I wanted my mother in my kid's lives. I wanted them to have a sense of family and to have that connection. I really thought I was doing a good thing and during this time it did seem like I was.

We eventually brought our things out from Missouri and our little house in the jungle became a home. The neighborhood was less than acceptable but we made due with the circumstances. Not more than a block to the east of us in a little dirt cul-de-sac lived the head of one of the biggest family gangs in Greeley. Their little boys along with the other kids that were allowed to roam the area would come and help themselves to the toys in our front yard. It didn't matter if my two sons were out there playing with them or not. I'd just look out and see them in my yard. Often I would shoo them away. They never cared to make friends with Zac and Jake. They just wanted their belongings. They were allowed to run loose and dirty. They had no respect for people's property.

One day while my husband was out working in the yard one of the little rascals walked up and flat out told him, "Your Wife is a bitch!"

Without flinching Scott replied, "Yeah, well she's my bitch." We still laugh about that.

It was next to impossible to get a nice lawn of grass to grow. Sand was everywhere as were the stickers and thorns. We succeeded in growing a front yard but the back yard was a lost cause. The house had a wood burning stove in it that was our primary source of heat. We had a huge waterbed in our room and so during the colder months the four of us slept in the heated bed together. We saved money by buying scrap wood from a contractor from construction sites. We would have large loads of end cut 2 by 4's and scrap pieces delivered and unloaded in the back yard. The pile of scrap lumber would be almost as high as or a little higher than the 6ft privacy fence that surrounded the yard. Our little mountain served two purposes, one as a heat source and two as the perfect hill to sled off of in the winter. For that matter the boys figured out how to do this year around. Only difference was instead of snow, in the summer they had the stickers that grew; this just added to the experience.

The house was coming along well, we had money, and my mother was back in our lives. Scott was working hard it was about this time that he had the opportunity to go pipelining. It was an opportunity that we had to take. Pipelining was in his blood and I knew that. He was successful and liked the work. So he took the offer knowing he was going to have to be careful not to fall in the rut again. And so for a while there seemed to be peace in the valley. Bills were paid and we had money and it seemed like we could dream again together.

THIRTY FIVE

The holidays came and went. The New Year 1994 brought with it a blessing I thought I would never have. Two sons had brought such joy and love into our lives. I had long since hung up any dreams I had of ever having a little girl. I hadn't given away my Barbie dolls and those things I had as a little girl, I hoped someday I could at least share them with a granddaughter. So when the thought occurred to me that I was pregnant I really didn't think it could be true. The home pregnancy test proved otherwise. I was in total shock! How was I going to explain this to Scott? I went from total elation to disbelief to being scared and then all of those feelings would hit me at once.

I wished I could say every time I told Scott I was pregnant that it was a joyous occasion; a moment that made us both jump up and down without a care in the world. Such was not the case for any of our babies. Scott may have been a lot of things but he took his parenting seriously. His own upbringing and relationship with a father that was absent physically and emotionally never left his memory. Joyce, his mother raised all six of the kids the best way she could, mostly without him.

It was more like a matter of fact kind of moment. There were never hugs and kisses and all that mushy stuff you see on the TV commercials. Professional pregnancy pictures weren't even thought of at that time. There wasn't any big announcement on social media. I was just pregnant and except for that our lives carried on.

Knowing all too well that the cost of having a baby in Colorado was going to be much more than in Missouri I began to make inquiries as to what the going rate was. I called the office of the OBGYN I had when we lived in Greeley years before and was astonished at the amount they charged especially the amount they expected as a down payment and monthly payments prior to giving birth. I could not believe what I was being told.

Working on the pipeline was great money and even though things were a little more expensive in Colorado compared to Missouri our finances were going really well. However, the doctor bill and hospital bill was going to be a huge sum of money. The downside to working on the pipeline at that time was that health insurance wasn't as available as it should have been and having just moved to Colorado months before we really hadn't had a chance to consider looking into health insurance. Here I was knocked up and up against the wall. Do we pay the exurbanite price cash for all this or do I look into alternative options?

The financially smart decision and the responsible decision was to suck up my pride and look into what was basically Colorado's indigent care program. It was a program that provided health care to the uninsured/underinsured. The cost was dependent upon a sliding scale fee that was a certain percentage of your income. Doing this meant I had to go to the other side of the tracks to a healthcare facility called Sunrise Health Care Center. I did what had to be done and made the appointment.

I was not prepared for what I witnessed on my first visit. The people that worked there were very nice but the waiting room was full of crying babies, pregnant ladies and sick old people.

In a country where I am a majority the minute I walked into the clinic I became a minority.

I never understood why the term Mexican was thought to be a derogatory term. If you are from Mexico you are a Mexican, just like I am an American. I was the only white blonde haired woman in the building. I didn't care I was doing the right thing by not putting us in the poor house by taking on a load of debt that I could avoid.

My First appointment went rather well and my nerves were somewhat put to rest, that was until I was informed that it would be several months before I could see a doctor. I was already at least 2 months along this delay meant that I would not be receiving any prenatal care until I was at the end of my second trimester.

I just couldn't accept that fact, and I didn't. I never was one that just took someone else's shit and walked away. If there was a better way to do something I tried to help find it. If a wrong was being carried out I tried to fix it. I didn't want to be reactionary like my mother. I wanted to be proactive, bring about a positive change or result. I'm not saying I was always 100 percent successful but I tried. I Don't like playing dirty or whipping out any aces I have in the hole early in the game but I will if that's the direction it's going to go.

Some of the staff there at Sunrise was supportive of the situation, and why not? It was as frustrating for them to have to work in the environment that existed to help people in need but turned them away at the same time. It was suggested that I apply to be on the board of directors. I did just that. Making phone calls and getting names and information on how to apply to the board also, brought my medical situation to light and it was found out that part of the problem was a front desk scheduling girl who wasn't properly trained. Thankfully, the misunderstanding regarding my pre-natal appointment was corrected. That was great that it got handled but I already had my panties in a bind over this and I wasn't going to back down. After submitting my application and letter and what seemed like months of phone calls I was invited to attend a board meeting. 6 months pregnant, reeeaaaalllly pregnant, I went to my first board meeting. The next month I was officially voted in as a board member.

THIRTY SIX

Sunrise Community Health Center was a federally qualified health care facility. It had an estimated 3 million dollar budget at that time, if memory serves me right. Despite the federal designation the funding received from the feds was not enough to properly run the facility. Community support from the other side of the tracks was weak. And the relationship with the local Hospital was one purely of tolerance and could have been better if it wasn't topped with ignorance and pride. The board at Sunrise was reeling from some internal strife that split the board and also caused a long standing clinic executive director to resign. I came in at the end of all this and I never dug too deeply into the mechanics of why and how all that took place. My concern coming on to the board was to do some housecleaning.

From my own experience working in healthcare for a heart specialist in Maryville Mo, when I was pregnant with Zac and Jake, I knew how important the front desk was. It's your first interaction with the patient and can set the tone for the whole experience. A competent gal with a smile and some understanding would get you a lot further when there was an issue with insurance coverage, a bill or the all too often and too long waiting period till the doctor came to see you.

Sunrise was a busy, packed clinic every day. It led to short fuses and bad attitudes by both the patrons and the workers. And it needed to be changed. I wanted to make Sunrise a better place for everyone. With what little medical background and accounting experience I had I understood a lot of the information we were given as the board. This was just a sliver of what I was going to need to know about and so I learned a great deal during my time on the board. Our job as policy makers and enforcers to accountability to the feds for every penny of our budget to fundraising and community development I loved learning as much as I could.

 For the first few meetings I watched and I listened, I asked questions and I observed and got a feel for the kind of people I was serving with. The matter at hand when I came on board was to search and find a new executive director. Mother nature had other ideas for me and so, on a board night no less, September of 1994 I was in the hospital giving birth.

I knew our third child would be a girl, the ultra sound had proven me right. It didn't seem that anybody else believed me until Haley Katherine Cronk made her debut. Aside from the healthcare issue I dealt with for the most part my final pregnancy was the best one. Our lives were moving in a positive direction.

Scott would still stay out once in a while and drink with his buddies, I could deal with that. I didn't like it in the least. But I dealt with it. I always thought it was cruel and insensitive that he never asked if I wanted to go that he never realized even if I did that I just couldn't leave our kids and go off and get stupid. We were parents now and I was committed to doing right by my kids and it didn't involve that. It hurt me that he could just go off and not come home after work. He was the one losing out not me. I had two beautiful little boys and a precious baby girl that were my world. Everything revolved around them. Sure I was stressed and wore out and tired from being a mommy. But I knew the day would come when the tables would turn. I knew that when our children didn't need me

24/7 and had begun their own lives that I wouldn't depend on him so much either and that if he hadn't changed his ways by then, that while I would most likely never divorce my husband I would live my own life. And so for the next 10 years that was my private consolation. The day would come when I wouldn't need Scott for anything. For now I did, especially since we now had our little girl.

It's true we never really planned our children. I left all that up to God. I didn't work hard to get knocked up. As it turned out if I didn't do something to keep from getting knocked up, I was kind of a fertile myrtle. Each one of our babies was a blessing and a gift. They brought so much into my life and Scotts and if it hadn't been for them it may well could have ended differently for Scott and me.

When tempers flare and feelings are hurt people do silly stupid things. You hurt so much that you want the other person to hurt too. Words are said things are done that can never be taken back. I was guilty of this, I'm human not a one of us is immune. If you are a one-sided person with tunnel vision, the 'it's all about me' type individual, then a relationship isn't something you're ready for. Because you would no doubt feel like it's you extending the most and being the better person than your mate. But if you are the kind of person that realizes that there is two sides to every story and that personal perceptions aren't always something that is shared; you will understand that the other person also feels like they are being the better person if they are truly trying. The things that I did, say or the way I behaved that would cause my husband to feel he had to compromise with me are things he may never have expressed to me. Just like I would do the same for him it's the give and take of a relationship.

My pregnancy with Katy went rather well as did the birth. I will always look back with some fondness at that time because it was a time I shared that was special with my mother. It was the first time when she could be there and be a part of the pregnancy. It was my mom that spent the day with me as my labor progressed and she also drove me to the hospital. She never left my side and it meant a lot to me that we could share those memories. We called Scotts work before we left for the Hospital, so shortly after checking in he was there as well. My kid sister stayed at the house and took care of the boys for me. Katy was my mother's first grandchild she got to see come into this world. It really was a great time. It was a shame it didn't last forever.

Katy was a month old when she attended her first board meeting. The other board members just adored her. And as we would go through the business for the night's meeting I would nurse her when she was hungry and rock her in her car seat as she slept. This beautiful little creature God had trusted me with was the very reason I was there. Being pregnant with her brought me to Sunrise.

THIRTY SEVEN

Diplomacy and tact, I would like to think I posses it. Possession is the operative word. I may have possessed it but didn't know how to deploy it. I have always felt that being upfront was a better approach than bullshit. I'm not one for pomp and circumstance. My own wedding video will prove that. I learned a lot about diplomacy and tact serving on the board for Sunrise. I also had a great mentor. The board chairman was a gentleman who took me under his wing and taught me how to lead and how to encourage teamwork. By his own actions he taught me how to really be a productive and beneficial board member. I was naïve and didn't realize that he was really grooming me to move up on the board.

Members could serve two 3 year terms before they had to resign. You could come back after a year if there was an opening and you were voted back on. I had served my first three year term and in that time had participated in everything I could do to help benefit the clinic and to streamline services. When my second term was voted on and approved it came with a promotion I was voted on as vice chair of the board. That was a huge thing for me. I loved Sunrise and I wanted to help the people that came to us for care.

I could tell that when it came time for board meetings or activities that Scott seemed a little jealous of it. It was like he resented my effort to contribute. It was the only thing I did outside of the house. My days were made up of taking care of our children and this was my only personal activity. I needed it. I can't count the times I'd go to a board meeting with spit up on the shoulder of my blazer that I hadn't noticed till I got there. Even my vocabulary was elementary. Moo-moo was milk, baba was bottle, and all the other cutesy names for items every kids needs through the day. Plus it gave me a sense of accomplishment that I was volunteering my time for something that helped people. So even though this hurt me that he didn't feel the same way I did, I never stopped and I never hesitated to do more for the clinic if called to do so.

During those first four years we hired an executive director, accepted her resignation and hired another director, dealt with board strife and personnel issues, improved the way services were provided and worked tirelessly to improve our relationship with the community. Greeley was no different than any other town. The good ole boy network was alive and thriving. It even had a couple good ole gals that were calling the shots from behind the curtains. It sickened me that the two facilities that should be partnered up and working side by side were not. NCMC the local hospital board and sunrise had a rift between them that I never understood and quite frankly should never had existed to begin with but when you have a burr in your britches and you sit on bags of money I guess it doesn't matter to you whether the people who need your help are getting it or not because it's the principle of the matter. Even if it's not cost effective for your organization it's still the principle of the matter. As far as I was concerned the good ole boys needed to be booted out of town on the nag they rode in on. Their mentality caused the pond to stagnate and poisoned everything.

THIRTY EIGHT

Weld County, Colorado is an agricultural area. Onion farms, lettuce, potatoes, beets are all gown in Weld County. This produce doesn't make it to market magically; it gets there through long days, low pay and the aching backs of the migrant workers that follow the growing season. As is with any culture you always have the scum at the bottom and the cream at the top. Living in Greeley and seeing the Mexican gangs, the kids that hang out and cause trouble or act like America owed them something and not like they had to earn their place like everyone else, it's real easy to get an impression of the migrant workers that isn't the most becoming.

It was decided at a board meeting that it would be beneficial for us to understand those we mean to serve during the growing season. Each board member would go out with the medical team when they did their outreach to the migrant camps. As is mandated by the feds our board had to be made up of a representation of those we served in the community. We already had two prominent board members who either came from a migrant family or grew up around the fields. How I got on the board was as a consumer board member meaning that I received my healthcare from Sunrise Community Health Center. However, I had no migrant experience. I gladly jumped at the opportunity to go and it changed my life.

It was a summer evening, driving my suburban I followed an old beat up station wagon down the dusty dirt back roads of

Weld County. Roads I never knew existed that turned into even more remote dirt roads I would never travel alone on. Meandering through corn fields and onion fields eventually the road would open up to a clearing. There were young men leaning against dilapidated sedans and old pickup trucks drinking beer. It was way past supper time. The sun was sinking on the horizon as we made it to this particular camp. If we wanted to see as many people as we could we had to be out late. When you farm its dawn to dusk and for the migrants this was never truer. There wasn't any grass for the kids to play in, just dirt and more dirt. The building these families called home was an 8plex, 4 apartments top and bottom. To me it looked like the farmer built it himself but it was their home. 8 different families young and old with or without kids all lived in this building.

I was the new girl, the only blonde in the group so I got stared at a lot just because I looked out of place. Before entering each home I was introduced and asked permission to come in with the team. It was a very humbling experience. The first home I entered was an older couple, retirement age but still working the farms. I was amazed here we were in the middle of nowhere in a shithole building and this one apartment couldn't be any more spic and span. It was immaculate. It was still a dump but it was a clean dump. The older couple couldn't be more welcoming.

The next apartments were young couples some with babies. But each place was clean. Each family had their own decorating tastes some were real young and loved the tapestries and traditional cultural décor. While other couples benefited from free carpet and items they found or bought at the thrift and pawn shops. Not at one of them had a bank account but they worked hard for their money and they did the best they could with what they had. I was shocked when I found out that farmer had the nerve to charge these people rent to live in his building. It really should have been condemned but it was their home.

Alcohol and drugs have no economic boundary. Neither is it color blind or in any way is selective. It will steal any soul it can and does it rather effectively. In poverty it seems to be the worst. It's a temporary escape from a life that is nothing but one hardship after another every single day. It leads to domestic violence and during the early 90's it was nothing to see an article in the paper that was about a Mexican couple getting in a fight and the woman wouldn't press charges so the guy gets out of jail and then kills her either by beating her to death or shooting her.   As we were visiting this camp I met a woman whose husband was abusive. She felt she had no other choice but to tolerate it, that she was subordinate to him, and so she wouldn't leave him or go to a shelter. What a terrible prospect to face so far away from home and feel so alone.

Many of the workers followed the growing season across the United States, some stayed in Greeley year round and some went back to Mexico. It was their life and they knew how to survive in it. I didn't have much myself, starting over again and this time with a new little baby. But I had more than they did and it made me feel spoiled. I witnessed the best and the worst of mankind that night. And I will never forget it.

Lots of good things and good changes were made for Sunrise when I served on the board. We had a great group of people that although we may not have saw eye to eye on all matters, each member's input was valued and respected. It was our differences that made us a great group. I learned some hard lessons on getting caught up in petty politics and I was even absent mindedly guilty of circumventing board policy when we had an issue with our staff. But I stand behind what I did, my mentor wasn't happy about it but when your chain of command is broke and it's that chain of command you must go through than how can a problem get fixed? Our staff had issues with the facility director and I chose to listen to their grievances. I made no apologies and in the end it all worked out. I ended up becoming board chair my last two years of service. It was a great six years I learned, I grew and I loved every minute.

THIRTY NINE

The anticipation and birth of our Katy added to what I thought was going to be a forever blissful life with nothing but good fortune ahead. Scott and I still had little tiffs nothing big for a young couple with kids. I could mark on a calendar, every 6 months or so he'd stay out all night without any word or warning. I just learned to cope with it by spending money or having some big house project waiting for him to complete once he got over his hangover. I didn't like it one bit. I knew he was drinking after work with the guys but I wasn't that big of a deal to me. It was when he didn't come home that I was so deeply hurt. How could he not want to come home to me if he loved me? Yet our life together was good and my life was full with three kids.

By the time Haley was three years old things started to slide downhill. Scott was carrying on more with people I never met or knew. Out of the blue a company called Will Bros called him; a longtime friend of ours had given them his name to see about working overseas. It was Venezuela and would be for 3 months. So I pimped my husband out to go overseas. We weren't getting along and I just couldn't deal with it. So he took the job and two weeks later the kids and I were waving goodbye to him at the airport. There wasn't any long embrace or lingering kisses. It seemed like he was anxious to be gone. He had no time for romance nonsense. I remember watching his plane taxi to the runway and feeling in my gut that I would never see him alive again. My brother in law Robbie just held me as I sobbed I never let on that was why I cried.

With Scott gone I had the best of both worlds. Bills paid money in the bank and no worries about whether or not my husband would be home for dinner. Five grand a month tax free, damn good money for those days. I missed the man I married, but not the man I put on the plane. Things were more structured at home and easy going. I didn't have to worry if Scott was going to come home in a bad mood or not come home at all. The kids and I did what we wanted and something I hadn't counted on happening happened. I seemed to be unstressing from having to be on guard all the time with Scott at home. The relationship I had with my mother was still in the positive side of the gauge and so we did many things together with my little sister.

It was time to move the family out of the ghetto. Time to leave the jungle, so I hired a contractor to build us a house in a little town called Windsor. Our business relationship was short lived, my realtor told him what we pre-qualified for which was a lot more than I wanted to spend; yet he was determined to help me spend it. I wasn't going to be house poor so I fired him and my realtor. New construction was nothing but a pain in my butt. I found another realtor and together we found the house I would have contracted and ready to sign on when Scott returned.

Throughout his absence Scott and I would write and the kids would send letters. It was my primary goal at all times that never should the kids be aware of mom and dad having issues and no matter what their dad would be prominent in their life's. It meant something to me to do this for not only the kids but my husband. Even when he wasn't there I always signed cards and such with love mom and dad. We had the usual I miss you letters but I wasn't stupid. I'm sure he had time off and when he did he was with the guys drinking or whatever.

It was a big pipeline, 36 inch oil pipeline down the Venezuelan hillside cutting through rainforests where howler monkeys lived and exotic birds flew. Not to mention the huge snakes and crocodiles. The experience was a once in a lifetime one for him. I've seen the pictures and heard some of the stories I have no doubt I haven't heard all of the stories and that's probably for the best. When the job was done and he flew home. The track record of shitty reunions continued. It was not what I had hoped for or expected in any way.

It would be a change for all of us, the stress free home the kids and I enjoyed was coming to an end, dad was home and we were getting ready to sign the papers for the new home I found for us. I was still hopeful and so I just kept praying and hoping.

FORTY

Our ranch style home was beautiful. It had a professionally landscaped yard with custom cabinets in the Kitchen and a nice big deck. It was something I had dreamed of for a long time. I knew this was our home when I saw the cherry wood cabinets and the Subzero frig. I never liked Greeley Colorado, even as a kid. Yet it was where I had roots and despite the dislike we built a life there. My mother was a big part of the kid's life. I sucked up her behavior twerks for the sake of the kids and allowed and encouraged her involvement in their lives. I thought I was doing a good thing.

Scott was working locally for the contractors we knew over the years. He was making good money and we seemed to settle into a middle class lifestyle. Still working long hours and often out of town, it was mostly just the kids and I. After some forays in self-employment I shrugged the stress of ownership and took a job at my alma mater, Greeley West High School.

My first year at GWHS was rocky. I was assigned to the guidance office. There were four counselors and one of them happened to be a teacher I had when I was a student there. She was one of my favorite teachers from those years; however, working with her was an absolute nightmare. I never quite could figure out whether she hated me because I told her she was my favorite teacher when I was in school and knowing how old I was that made her even older and longer in the fang than she wanted to admit or if she was just an overbearing dominatrix hell bitch. She made me extremely nervous, I never felt anything I did was good enough, and she was constantly bearing down on me. I was good at my job but she made me doubt myself so much that I made mistakes I normally wouldn't make had I not been stressed by experiencing her constant scrutiny. It was a relief when, despite her attempts to get me fired, I just ended up getting offered a new position and with more money.

 The next school year, when time came for the annual secret pal drawing, our office jokes of who the last person I should draw would be turned into a reality. I was asked if I wanted to redraw a name but I decided that I would keep my secret pal. I surprised her and pampered her with things I knew she would like. A hand full of people knew I had her for a pal. The anticipation was building for the day we revealed ourselves... The shock on her face when she found out it was me was priceless... I don't know if she learned anything from it but I walked away knowing that I was the better person.

Being the better person; what a task that can be. I have always tried to be that way, sometimes with success sometimes not. The point is I always tried. I would continue to take hits for the home team if I thought it was beneficial for my family and kids. The problem was that I was stupid and should have stood up sooner. A lesson was waiting just around the corner for me that forever changed my life and would forever be a part of jaded and dark past I cringe to even tell the story. Success always comes at a price. Our success was costly. Scott never ever lacked motivation or drive. He always wanted more for his family to provide more for our kids. Unfortunately, unresolved issues from his past before we met always haunted him and it made him unpredictable and irrational. When combined with the drive to be more and do more the result was a sort of Molotov cocktail.

The goodness in my husband was shrouded over by darkness once again. It was a slow decent, first coming home later and later then finally not at all for days. When I would see him it was always very tense on both our parts. I didn't understand why he was doing what he was doing and the longer it went on the more hurt I got.

Smoking pot is one thing. It dulls your wits in moderation I have no problem with it. But if you have an addictive personality it's just a life sucking drug. Meth on the other hand is a plague on mankind. It is an insidious evil that steals your soul and replaces it with nothing. You're just a dying shell. For whatever reason I do not have an addictive personality, I can stop as easily as I start. It is the only reason why I didn't do drugs all the time. When Scott and I first got together I loved to party and I did. First smoke a little pot then I did my first line of cocaine in 1985 with a rolled up hundred dollar bill. Later on I dropped some acid and took a few trips on mushrooms. I didn't like surrendering myself to a Hallucinogenic. To lose self-control and not know for sure what you're seeing is real or not just wasn't my thing. Speed was a great way to get shit done. The bad part about that was coming down from it. It was nothing to stay up for three days and dream and make big plans and fool around... but then when the crash came all those big ideas would be gone and you were still stuck in your living room really cranky and really tired and wishing you had bought more.

I enjoyed smoking a little pot and when the chance came up I'd do some speed, but I never needed any of it. As our marriage started to deteriorate again I smoked pot to just keep from hurting I'd do it in the bedroom when the kids weren't around. When I had some it was nice when I didn't then I just didn't. No big deal. When I was sick, and dealing with what would ultimately result in a total hysterectomy, it was the pot that helped me the most with managing my pain. I knew Scott was using again. I had no idea to what degree. On the occasions when he would come home if he had some speed with him I'd do it with him. I'm not sure if it could be called codependency, but it helped us get along when he was around. That's why I did it. The stress was incredible. The tension between us was crushing. I knew Meth was taking my husband from me and it seemed like he didn't even care. I tried to make do the best I could. I went to every extent to hide it all from the kids. It would be awfully naive to think they didn't sense something was wrong. To this day I haven't asked. I can't bring myself to do it. I am so ashamed I wasn't strong enough to stand up sooner and stop it. Even knowing now after all these years how it all worked out I still am ashamed that I wasn't strong enough.

FORTY ONE

Scott wasn't your usual addict, he may have had the devil on his back but he never once stopped providing for his family and so all the way up until the catastrophic end we always had money. Money of which was spent on family camp trips, cabin rental in the Rockies, road trips, kids parties and just living a good life despite the revolving front door my husband entered and left through.

He had his friends and I had mine. The only friend I needed was a crazy lady who would become a fellow Chica Momma. The year Katy was in kindergarten she befriended another little girl. During the school year they became good friends. On occasion I would see her mother and we'd share small talk. At one point her and her husband needed a concrete pad poured to set their hot tub on and they hired the company I was part owner of to do the work.

I was so busy just living, that looking for a friend wasn't on my radar. I am eternally grateful that it was on hers. On a hot summers day this crazy women with a walking boot on one leg, a big thermal sippy jug in one hand a couple hippie braids in her hair and these wicked long colored nails comes knocking on my door out of the blue. We have been inseparable ever since. It has been one of my most cherished blessings that God brought Tammy into my life.

Over the years our families have grown together and grown up. She is unconditionally accepting and genuine. She is unique and fun and I love her to death, she is my soul sister having her in my life has been nothing short of marvelous and stupendous all rolled up and wrapped with my undying gratitude and love.

Together and then later on with another dear friend Ronnie, our kids became the Chicas. We had such great adventures and stories that could fill a book on their own. They are some of my favorite memories.

My marriage kept sliding downhill but with Tammy in my life it really didn't seem that bad. Our houses where just a short distance from each other, we had this route worked out that kept us from driving on the busy roads to each other's house. I called it the Scooby Doo bypass. It was like one big commune our kids would go back and forth sometimes they'd all be at my house, sometimes hers others half and half. It was good for the kids and good for us too. On the occasion Scott was home we got along a little better just because I finally had some distraction from my sucky life and marriage. Our problems were still there and they were getting worse.

Scott had several friends who I considered the bane of my existence. They partied hard, drank, did drugs and lord knows what else I didn't know about. Through the years we have lost friends and seen others incarcerated. One of our friends will be lucky to experience freedom in just 17 more short years. Another friend ended up dying from carbon monoxide poisoning. He supposedly passed out in his truck while it was running in his shop. His death was a shock. The day of his funeral the church was packed. Afterward we held a proper pipeliner send off at his place. A huge bonfire lots of booze and whatever else. Despite the little fucker being a pain in my ass, we did have a love hate relationship. His death really sucked. He left behind a longtime girlfriend. We may have all been one dysfunctional group of people, but we came together when it counted and so Scott was among a few pipeliners that tried to see that she was taken care of. She was capable of taking care of herself but in her grief it was a very sweet gesture that had it been me I would have appreciated it, I know she did and so at the time it didn't bother me.

Weeks wore on Scott was gone more and longer. Promises to be home went unfulfilled and I was left at home crying and hurt. Eventually I got to where I was going to stand up for myself and when the kids were asleep late in the night I would drive the 15 miles or so to the place she lived and sure enough Scott's truck would be there. When his buddy died he had a shop and tools, equipment and a couple welding rigs he left behind. Scott had been using the shop to do some fabrication work. He also had taken his personal duty to look after the girlfriend a little further than I thought he should have. It seemed like he cared more for her than his own family. I never caught him being unfaithful just stupid. After working all day he'd work in the shop at night, get drunk or messed up and end up staying at her house.

I finally had enough and would drive over there and confront him late in the night. Pounding on the door demanding that he come out, just so freaking hurt and embarrassed that I had to track my husband down at another woman's house. Sometimes I would be so hurt I'd just slug him or slap him, he'd always take it. I never really knew why. At one time I had him out by his truck. I grabbed him by his t-shirt and took him to the ground tearing the shirt. I was going to give as good as I got. I took his truck keys and threw them way out in the field and left. So many times he was the aggressor, this time I had the drop on him. What's more I didn't care if he would have beaten me. At least then I would look the same on the outside that I felt on the inside.

Tracking him down was an infrequent thing I did, I always waited for the kids to be asleep then I'd find him. He had several places to go. I would make a best guess at which one he was at. Most times I was dead on. I just hurt so much that I wanted him to see how much I hurt. I wanted it to make a difference to him. I wanted it to click in his head that what we had was a good thing once. In the end I always came back alone and hurting more.

For several years I lived like this. Scott would come and go he would fit in our life when he wanted to. When it came to the kid's birthdays' and events like that he was always there. If I planned a trip he would go and we would pretend it was good and then we'd come home and he'd be off in his world. I never knew if something was going to make him mad it seemed like he was always tense and mad. Sometimes I would look in his eyes and just see rage. So I did the best I could to keep things defused around him.

It got so that when he had to go on location out of town on a job that I was thankful. At least I knew for sure he wouldn't be home at night. It drastically reduced the tension and some of my stress. As long as the checks hit the bank and bills were paid I was good.

FORTY TWO

I prayed constantly, every night for God to bring back my husband, for my family to be ok and for the kids to not be affected by all of this. I tried to keep my tears to myself and my heart ache. I always was vigilant that their father wasn't bad mouthed by me. I did everything I could possibly think of to insulate them from all of it. But I was getting to the end of my rope.

As Scotts struggle with the meth monkey on his back began to overpower him ,my desperation and decent into the scariest place I have ever been was only overshadowed by my determination that the kids not catch on to my own private struggle. The countless nights I spent alone crying in our room I'd pray, "Lord please give me the strength to carry on, please help me do the right thing, please bring my husband back to me. Lord, be there for our children keep them safe and hold them in your merciful hands. "
It was the same prayer I prayed every night, every day, all the time.
I loved life, loved to feel life. In the fall I would sit out on our back deck and in the crisp silence of an autumn evening I could literally hear each leaf snap from its branch. The crunching sound as it would bounce off the other tree limbs on its way to the ground in tandem with other leaves was like an acoustic nature symphony.
In the winter I would take the kids to Hidden Valley Ski resort just outside of Estes Park and we would sled down the slopes. The winter wonderland that opened itself to us as we would trek into the hills was covered in white, pristine beauty...

breathtaking beauty.   Snow blanketed pine trees covering the mountains that stood as silent sentinels around us. A low hanging winter mist that danced across the tree tops, hinting at the possibility that more snow could be on the way. The air fresh, cold and invigorating; I couldn't take enough deep breaths, it was exhilarating to me. It didn't matter what season it was winter, spring, summer, or fall the mountains were where I felt closest to God.

Summers were spent at North Fork way up the Poudre Canyon past the Red Feather Lakes and Killpecker Ridge we would spend our weekends and vacations as a family camping, nestled among the lodge pole pines right next to the river. Level 6 roads for the last 10 miles or so before getting to our destination. That meant the road maybe got graded once a year. It was rustic to say the least. We packed out what we packed in. During the days we hiked and trekked deeper in the mountains; going up to Dead Man's tower, a ranger outpost that is used to spot forest fires. The tower overlooked endless panoramic miles of the canyon.

In the evenings as dusk would settle in I would sit sipping on a toddy as the amber glow from our campfire would highlight the shadows of the surrounding timber, a wonderful woodsy smell of pine filling the air, I would sit back in my camp chair looking up to the sky surrounded by these giant trees that reached to the heavens. I would watch as they would sway in the evening breeze that blew way above us where the tree tops were. This was God's house. I raised my kids telling them that God's house was where nature and beauty and true creation resided. I felt all these things and more, I felt them to my core, they were what made me.

The night I realized I couldn't feel life anymore I was devastating. I wondered if I had passed a point of no return. It was my own Hell. It was like all the sound was sucked out of my world. I no longer lived, I just existed in a vacuum surrounded by a barrier that cruelly let me see the world and its splendor but when the trees swayed in the breeze.. I couldn't feel it. When it rained... the scent of renewal and the aroma of spring flowers were non-existent. I functioned everyday not letting on how much I was hurting. My kids were the only thing I had that offered any temporary respite.

At night as I would lie alone in bed, the result of another broken promise from Scott that he would be home, I would wonder what good could I possibly be to my own children. I never contemplated suicide but I was completely ok with the thought that if God called me home in my sleep, it would have been a release. Every morning that I woke up I took it as another chance to get it right, obviously, the good Lord was trying to teach me something and I wasn't catching on.

My biggest moment of shame as well as a blessing in disguise was about to happen and believe it or not it was an answer to all the years of prayers I had prayed. Tension between Scott and I had now reached a level of intensity that I hated him. I hated him and I loved him. I hated him for everything he had done to destroy, again, every dream I thought we had, and every hope of ever attaining goals I thought we shared.

He came home unpredictably, one evening in May of 2003, probably to just take a shower, eat and leave again. The exact reason I don't know. I was in the living room with our daughter and he overheard me discipline her and didn't like it. I had enough of this tyrant I called a husband and I went in to the kitchen to have it out with him. Words were said exactly what words I don't remember but I do know what about and it dealt with him never being home and being a junkie.

Round one ended up with him taking me by the collar of my shirt and pushing me up against the door to the garage. As I slid down the door the door knob dug into my back by the time it reached my shoulder blade the knob had sheared off and what was left of the jagged part on the door tore into my flesh. I never felt it happen. I got up and went to get our daughter and the daughter of a good friend of ours who was spending the day with us and headed them to the front door. At that time my mother was walking up to the door and I quickly opened it and told her to take all the kids and to call the cops.

Calling the police was a big deal for me. I knew by taking that step I was finally saying it's time to end this, I knew that there would be involvement that was out of my control. I didn't know to what extent but at that time I felt it was the right thing to do. As my mother drove off with the kids I turned around and went back into the house. Asking and begging Scott to tell me what had gotten into him, only to be met with replies that where unfathomable, calling me names and not making any sense. I couldn't handle it anymore I just let him have it. I told him what a dumb fuck he was and what a no good junkie he was and that I knew he was a better man than that. We kept exchanging words. He tried to unholster the 9mm Beretta he carried on his belt and it misfired. The bullet put a hole in our kitchen floor about twelve inches from my big toe. I wasn't even fazed. I knew it was an accident but secretly wished he would have just put me out of my misery. He wasn't unholstering the gun to shoot me but it went off nonetheless.

We continued to argue, I mean really why not? I knew the cops would be on their way soon. He grabbed me by the throat, I could feel his grip. I didn't put up a fight I told him to go ahead and kill me because I was already dead inside. He let up I knew at that point we had nothing else to say to each other so I got my truck keys and walked out the door. Scott followed me all the way to my suburban, I struggled to get in and as I shut the door he hit it with his fist leaving a dent. I backed out the driveway and drove around the block. When I drove back onto the street we lived I pulled over at the corner and watched the cops pull up.

My mother drove up to me with the kids. I was horrified that she did that... they needed to be away from this... I told her to leave and I would handle this, she got huffy and left. Was a dumb thing to do on her part. Within minutes the Police called me on my cell. I told them I was in the red suburban at the end of the block and they drove up to meet me. I had to tell them for their own safety that there were guns in the house, I didn't want Scott shot but I didn't want anyone else shot either. I told them a little bit about what happened and then they called the swat team in. I gave them Scott's cell number and they established communication with him.

Thank God after about 20-30 minutes they talked him out. I stayed where I was parked. I could see a little bit of what was going on mostly the activity of all the cops running around like it was a field day at the circus. I know Scott had to come out the front doors with his hands up and lay prone on the yard before they cuffed him. I know this but I didn't see it and I wouldn't be able to bear seeing it. How scared and lost he must have been, at least the Scott I knew deep inside must have been. The Scott they were dealing with was rage filled and nothing but a meth monster.

After Scott was taken away I drove up to the house and went inside. The aftermath of our argument was visible, a hole in the wall, a broke bed and a sheared off door knob. Sitting at the dining room table, while I was talking with the officers they went through the whole house. They continuously asked me if I was scared for my life and I repeatedly told them "No!"... It got on my nerves. I kept saying that it wasn't my husband that did all this. "That wasn't the Scott I knew". They kept up their effort to get me to say I was scared but I never caved. I wasn't ever scared. I was pissed at Scott for being a dumb shit. I was hurt so deeply that my own spirit was gone and all I had was an empty soul. I was shocked that I finally had to resort to this and then look where it got me...being questioned by cops who were out to get my husband NOT help him. They were trying to coerce me into saying something to help them along their personal mission. As I was deflecting their attempts I caught them walking out with my guns, the guns that I had inherited from my dad and I was having none of it. I stopped them and asked them what they were doing. Their reply was taking them for my safety. That was a bunch of shit, and they knew it. I told them to put the guns back, every one of them. They were mine and weren't going anywhere. The cops had to turn around and put them back. The police did confiscate the guns that were Scott's and that was only right.

In the process of searching my home under the guise of making it "safe" they found my glass pipe and case. It had been months since I quit smoking but I kept the pipe because it was a gift from someone special to me, now it was confiscated. They asked me if I smoked pot my honest reply was no but nonetheless they now had an item I kept out of sentimental reasons and would be the reason I would be drug tested later on.

 When they finished tearing my house up further and left I was still sitting at the table in shock. Scott was in jail and now I had to go make sure my kids were ok and try to do some damage control. I let them stay with my mom, not unlike any other summer night and I went to my friend's house and slept on an air mattress in her living room. In the morning her daughter came to check on me and noticed the hand marks on my neck, later on in a letter to the prosecuting attorney they would write about this. Grateful that morning had come, I got up and thanked them for their kindness and left.

I had no plan but to check on the kids and then get the house fixed so I could bring the kids home to something other than a war zone. I looked terrible, puffy face, sore body and my right shoulder was aching and hurting terribly. My collar bone was broken. As Scott threw me against the door he had me pinned with his forearm bracing against it and it broke. I didn't know it was broken at that time. It wouldn't be till years later that I realized that it had been broken and the only reason why was because it showed up in an x-ray I had taken of my shoulder for other reasons. The night previously, I refused medical treatment I didn't see the need in it. I knew by doing so it would have been used against Scott.

Let me clear the air here, I absolutely hate the word martyr. One thing that intensely irritates me is when my husband thinks it's cute to say "Mother and Martyr, two words that start with M"... I am not a martyr. I am on the other hand, no dummy either. I would be lying if I said I didn't know why I had the foresight to do the things I did or say the things I said that were in the best interests of my family during this time. I was in damage control mode for my children's sake first and our family. I was constantly vigilant of how things could be used against Scott that would deflect from the fact that he needed help. He wasn't a hardened criminal, he may have been a rough character to others but I knew he was better than that. I knew he needed help. I was scared that this would finally be the end of us as a married couple. I was prepared to give it my best effort to see that didn't happen so that if he walked on his own that I could honestly say to myself and the

"Almighty" that I tried my best. I could never walk away from a solemn promise I made to God without doing so.

FORTY THREE

For once in my life I didn't have the bull by its horns; on the contrary I was hanging on for dear life trying to make the ride. So every move I made was made carefully and with lots of prayer well almost everyone. I did kick a social services lady off my doorstep for showing up unannounced.

The next two days I spent getting the house back in order as the kids stayed with their grandmother. I also needed the time to get myself back in the game. My face was still puffy and the marks hadn't disappeared from my neck yet. I had my best friend come over and help me, she was speechless and didn't know what to do or say. I couldn't say anything it was all beyond words at that point. So she went home. I got the house lined out and brought the kids home. A new era of great uncertainty began.

As much as I wanted to be there at the arraignment just to see Scott, I knew it would make no difference to him; he was probably still pissed over the whole deal. It was only a couple days or so after the fight that the arraignment took place I still looked horrid. I didn't need to prove the prosecution's case for keeping him in jail. Plus I figured it sent a message that I had enough of his shit. I didn't bail him out either. His "friend" from Johnstown did. As far as I was concerned at that time, they deserved each other. I also figured I was probably taking a chance of chasing him into her arms but then again, if that was the case than, I clearly didn't need him in my life. Everything was up in the air. I focused on the kids and keeping a routine during the day. At night I prayed, I cried and I never felt the world coming in on me more than I did at that time, and it was about to get worse.

Because of a Colorado law an immediate order of protection was placed against Scott so that he/we couldn't have any contact. I didn't want it, in fact I vehemently argued against it. How were we to arrange for paying the bills and handle affairs of that nature if we couldn't talk? I didn't so much care about him not living at home. I didn't want him home. He was living in our camper trailer in Johnstown. The prosecuting attorney's response was that I could get victims assistance to "help" pay the bills… here is where the absolute idiocy of it all comes to play. I could get assistance through this and then they would bill Scott. Okay so let's see, they are going to bill Scott to give me assistance to pay necessary bills. Not all the bills. FUCK THAT!!!   I told them that was ridiculous and walked out. So Scott and I eventually established contact for that purpose we continued to handle our finances despite the court order that I never wanted. I still to this day resent that I was denied the right to choose for myself and was treated like the weaker sex and a dummy. Truly for as much good that exists in our government system there is just as much and more idiocy and waste both in process, laws and the people that uphold them.

Our relationship was very matter of fact. Whatever was between us was one thing but our kids were another and we still came together as we always have for them.

Dealing with having to sneak around some protection order was difficult enough, just when I thought things were settling down a little and I could breathe some; I got an unexpected visit from a social services/child welfare lady.

I'm not a "It takes a village to raise a child" kind of gal. My private business is mine alone unless I share it with you; my family business is even more sacred. I don't tolerate interference by do-gooders who may or may not have authority and who may or may not misuse that authority to my disadvantage. I guess in short you could say I don't trust anyone…. And you would be right! So this poor gal comes to visit me on a sunny day as I am redecorating my bathroom, the kids are in the living room watching a TV show, she knocks on my door and is quickly and effectively told to leave. She obliges and then I quickly get a hold of an attorney. This is one guy who I should use his name because he sucked so terribly as counsel that everyone should know who not to hire. Anyways, he served his purpose in my life although briefly and long enough to tell me without knowing the case in whole that I was going to lose my kids. Ohhh yeah and I had to play nice with social services. I was now scared out of my mind and devastated for my kids. Their life did not deserve to be turned upside down any more than it had, regardless of the damage control both their father and I had done to keep them from the nastiness of what had happened. And all because we couldn't get our shit together! No amount of pride was worth ever losing my kids!

So I sucked up my pride and called the lady back and invited her to come for a visit. Inviting her to visit gave me a sense of having some control over the situation. Something I had nothing of until this point and really still didn't but I felt that way anyways. The division of child services and the criminal court system now really ruled my life. Fortune smiled a little when we drew a very nice young gal as our initial social worker. She had a job to do and I knew that but she could have been some snooty lady with a chip on her shoulder. You know like the kind that had a crappy childhood and now are social workers crusading to right the wrongs they were subjected too. This gal was different, I was adamant as was Scott that while the kids' welfare was primary that as far as the facts where concerned, they were not to be told. We did this for several reasons; first being that they were still young and didn't need to carry the burden of that knowledge. The second reason was that we felt the exposure to knowing drugs were involved would set the bad example in their life that they would follow. The final reason was that we did not want them to feel shame for poor decision making on both our parts. While our relationship started off on rocky ground with the case worker, she did respect our wishes and we ended up working very well together.

FORTY FOUR

Scott and I now had two fronts to fight; his criminal deal and now we had family services to deal with. We hired a bulldog attorney to represent him on the criminal side and this guy's partner would represent Scott in family services court. I would go without representation. I was advised to get a lawyer but chose to go it alone.

We had an emergency family court to address the kid's welfare. Scott showed up with his attorney. I showed up with my mother in tow. While we couldn't be together I could see him on the stairs a level above me, we made eye contact and he winked at me. It was an "everything will be ok wink". For the last month we had established communication and once again we were rebuilding our relationship. Scott was waking up from the meth madness that ruled his life and was trying to kick it on his own. He was slowly returning to the Scott I knew. He still had a long way to go but he had willpower and God what more could you want?

In court and I was awarded sole custody of the kids, again seemingly moronic. You see the courts address these things like they are hostile matters and ours wasn't. I guess we weren't your ordinary situation. I understand they had concerns for our kids. But I didn't need to be told I had sole custody of my own kids, that was obvious. We had a lady judge and I liked her. She presented herself as fair and unbiased yet with some compassion, I could sense it and it put me at ease. She ordered a drug test for both of us after awarding me custody and then some other precursory things like evaluations for each of us. I knew Scott would flunk. I hadn't done anything for months but was still nervous and was not about to just go pee in a cup I was going to make sure nothing tested "hot".

We each had 4 hours to report for testing so I remembered what one of our friends said about taking niacin and drinking a ton of water to test clean on a urinalysis. He said just take a handful, he meant a few I took it as literally a handful. After purchasing the niacin and a jug of water, I got in my truck, broke the seal, popped a handful of pills and drank a bunch of water. I sat there for a few minutes than started my truck, before I pulled out of the parking lot my butt started itching and feeling like it was on fire, than my arms and my legs, it was that quick. I got real scared. I thought to myself I should probably drive to the hospital. But then what am I going to say? "Hey I just took a handful of niacin to avoid testing dirty on a court ordered UA." Gee, I might as well drop my kids off at social services on my way there. NOT! No I figured I had got myself in this deal I would see it through. Before I could shut the front door of the house behind me I was puking yellow gunk on the carpet. I couldn't hold it back, it was projectile barf. It was all I could do to get to the toilet before the next round. My stomach was empty and I was still dry heaving. All the exertion had left me extremely weak. I could only hope that some of the niacin made it passed the puking. Sitting on the bathroom floor, I slugged as much water as I could without drowning. Finally, I started peeing like a racehorse. I was now a weak and drowned rat. I still had an hour to go before I had to report but I couldn't drink any more water and I stopped peeing. I decided to take my chances and pulled my carcass off the floor, walked to my truck and drove to the testing place.

I hated that place. As a matter of fact it was a place that had a rather unstellar reputation. But then why would they care. They were contracted and made a ton of money off of other people's addictions, people who were already frowned on by society so whether they were treated fairly or with respect didn't matter. I was prepared to draw some guy with an attitude but was equally as prepared to suck it up too. I was extremely relieved when the gal that helped me was really very nice. I was wearing my favorite suit and jacket that had a lovely shade of purple in it, which in turn accented the lovely shade of red that the niacin had turned my whole body. I looked like I had fallen asleep in the sun. When she commented on my sunburn and how it must hurt, I played along like I got it while I was outside working in my flower garden.

I was a little nervous when she had to watch me pull my pantyhose down and pee in the cup. I was glad to get it all over with. I got real nervous when she said the judge also ordered a "patch". I knew the judge ordered it for Scott but she didn't do it for me at least not in my presence. I was a little put off by the surprise but didn't let on. I had no choice but to get the damn thing, I would deal with how to make sure I pass that test after I got home.

The "patch", well at least they didn't order a hair follicle sample. I'd be dead meat if that were the case. A hair follicle sample would have detected usage for months and would have sunk my ship. While it would be hard to get a hair sample from a totally bald person, I mean stem to stern, guilt would have been obvious had I shaved. Of which I would have done most likely anyways and then force a "patch" but that was a hypothetical situation. The "patch" was my reality. It was relatively new to me I had never heard of it until that day. So I did some homework on it when I got home. I don't like uncertainty. I don't like being at the mercy of human error. The chances of me testing positive were very remote but I was still scared. I was not going to take any chances. The patch could be defective, errors on the lab side could happen. I had too much to lose not to make sure I came up on the sunny side of this deal.

The patch was a special type of large band aid that the gauze pad inside of it absorbed your body sweat and excretions. The idea is that your body sweats out the chemical signatures of the drugs you do. It's kind of like an insurance policy to a whiz quiz. The rules of this game were that you could not tamper with the patch in any way or it would be considered "hot" which meant positive for drugs. Even if after being tested it still was negative. It didn't matter if you worked outside in the sun and sweated a bunch and the thing came loose. They would just tell you not to work so hard that it comes loose. Forget whether or not it impedes your ability to make a living. You had to wear the darn thing for a week and then go back in to the testing place and have them remove it.

The whole week I wore it I fretted. I worried about how I was going to make this thing work in my favor. Finally, I came up with the deep cleaning my house and being concerned bleach or cleaning chemicals soaked through the patch, which kind of did, with a little help. A couple days before I had to go in to have it removed I carefully took a tooth pick and forced up an edge of the patch. Just enough to slip a q-tip with bleach on it through to the gauze pad. I saturated the pad with bleach and then used spray adhesive to seal the edge down again. When I went in to have it removed they were none the wiser for my dirty trick. It was kind of funny the person removing the patch commented on how difficult it was to get off. I just said I took extra good care of it and left it at that.

I walked out of the testing place breathing what would be the beginning of a sigh of relief. At least that was over with. I gave it all I had and then some to insure that my kids were not going to be sleeping anywhere but their own beds at night.

FORTY FIVE

A week later the case worker called me to say that all my tests came back ok, but Scott's didn't. Scott and I had talked about that and I was prepared for his news and very relieved for mine. It bears worth mentioning that in retrospect I highly doubt anything I did to avoid from testing positive really worked or did anything but shorten my life. But my trust issues got the better of me and so they ruled my reasoning abilities at the time. In the end I did what I felt needed to be done and I did it.

Trust in God. Three words that pack one heck of a punch. Those are huge words to live by and the most difficult for me. Sure I trust God but not mankind. That was the paradox of my then dilemma. After kicking the social worker off my doorstep and being told by a shitty attorney that I was going to lose my kids I nose-dived mach 5 into the gutter of despair. I couldn't be any lower mentally, spiritually and emotionally. I was unfathomably scared that I was really going to lose my kids. I sobbed just thinking of how that would go down and the thought of seeing them cry and be frightened destroyed me inside. When I got home from that "legal consultation" the kids were with their grandmother so I had the house all to myself. I remember collapsing in the comfy chair in the front room and I broke down.

I was nothing better than scum. I was worthless. I was broke beyond repair. I had no hope and I felt like I had already lost. Even though I was still fighting, the odds were against me for a fact and all I had was prayer. Sitting in that chair I placed my head in my hands and I prayed for one thing. "Lord please let my children be ok. Let them come out of this unscathed. Please, Lord keep my children from being hurt. Keep them safe." As I finished the last words of my prayer I felt an inner warmth growing, rising to my skins surface. I sat back in the chair and it was as if that warmth now was all around me. I felt at peace. I felt light, as if my troubles were lifted and my spirit was getting recharged at the same time. There was a serene, pure heavenly ray that shown down and surrounded me. Then I heard a man's voice, a deep voice a calm firm loving voice and it said, "Holly, your kids will be okay" as quickly as it came it left. Those few seconds changed my life forever. I sobbed uncontrollably it was like a release. Eventually I ran out of tears and when I got up from that chair I knew what I had to do. I had to humble myself, accept the involvement of others in my life and trust in God that it would be ok.

Obviously the drug testing thing happened soon after and I hadn't yet caught on to the humbling and trusting thing but I did continue to work on it and to work with the people who would be placed in my life whether I wanted them in it or not. And I would do this because this was how I, my kids, Scott and WE were going to be stronger in spite of the ugliness. God didn't tell me that the kids would end up with me. He didn't promise me anything other than they would be ok. That's what I prayed for; that they would be ok, where and how was going to be dependent on how I would handle the train wreck that was now my life, our life. I still didn't trust mankind but I had trust in God to make it right despite them.

FORTY SIX

Of all things, to find out that there is a betrayer among your innermost circle. One whom you trusted with your thoughts, plans, tactics and children is a hard thing to come to terms with when you're working to do the right thing and rebuild a life, a stronger better life. It's a betrayal that had it not been for knowing I was armored with God's love, I would have not been strong enough to battle.

The betrayal of a mother, my mother! I trusted her, Why shouldn't I? I needed my mother to be a mother. From the very first conversation I trusted her with about secretly meeting Scott and about the fact that despite putting my rifles in a safe at a friend's house I had kept my 38 chief for protection; my mother had been lobbying the prosecuting attorney's office and calling anonymously to social services.

Part of our family plan that we had with the family courts was to have ten visits with a therapist who would come to the house and help us talk about what was going on. She too was very professional and nice. We all liked her. I liked having her visit. After all the initial scare of them operating on the assumption we were the worst kind of human beings possible, they had figured out that Scott was really a good guy who just got lost in the meth madness and that our family really wasn't a high risk so we were ranked at the bottom of the scale. The family courts always treated us with dignity and respect.

During one of the meetings we had it was mentioned that they had been receiving numerous anonymous calls about us. Scott hadn't yet been cleared to come home. At least he couldn't be at the house when the kids were there. Surprisingly, by this time the court mandates were perfect for me so that they actually helped me get a backbone again. Scott couldn't come home to live until he tested three times drug free. It killed him to be away from us as a family and although he could come for the meetings that was it. So when the kids were at my girlfriend's house we would plan to meet at home. This anonymous caller would report those times among other things. It was obvious who it was by the reports being made and so I knew the betrayer was my mother.

Still fighting our battle with the criminal courts I would, on occasion, have the need to interact with the district prosecuting attorney. During a visit to his office I was point blank asked about my mother. Apparently, her forked tongue didn't spew venom to just social services. She had been calling the DA and had even written him a letter. When asked about her I just shrugged my shoulders, smiled and said she was emotionally disturbed. I knew she had already proven herself to be all that by their inquiry, hence the smile.

It was all very cordial with the DA, they had a job to do, I didn't agree with them wanting to put Scott away for 13 years or more but being anything but civil and a woman of integrity and honor would not get the results I wanted. There was no need for any behavior other than that when dealing with him, although, later I had a little fun with him when I testified. My mother unwittingly had actually helped our case despite her poison pen letter.

During the times when the kids would talk alone with our family counselor it came out that my dear ole ma was also badmouthing not just Scott but me as well to them. Degrading us and belittling us as parents. I was aware that she bad mouthed us to my sister but had no idea that she was freely and constantly doing this to our kids as well. The woman was throwing her own daughter under the bus. I don't know why I shouldn't have been surprised. She had a vocabulary and an attitude that she used like a surgeon uses a scalpel to operate with. Except she doesn't bother sewing up the wound she cut open.

FORTY SEVEN

I had enough, I felt I had backing to stand up to her and so I did. The weekend came and I knew she would want to see the kids. When she called I was so nervous I was shaking. But I knew I was doing the right thing. I could hear the tone in her voice. It just made my blood run cold. There was nothing there but her sense of entitlement. No respect for me, no love, nothing but the need to serve herself. I don't remember what she wanted to do with the kids. I do remember her response when I told her that I knew about her calls to social services and her letter and visits to the District Attorney of which she tried to deny. I went on tell her that until this whole legal matter was over and done with that she was not allowed to have any contact with the kids. She went berserk! I tried to stay calm it was hard because when she knew she had been had her voice escalated and all I heard were shrieks and screams and threats. I hung up. She called back at least three times after that I just let the machine pick it up. I stood there in the dark of my room and listened to her screaming; that voice the frantic manic tone that makes my skin crawl. It was pure evil and that was my mother.

Being the emotional volcano of selfness that my mother is she didn't stand down. She found out when our next family court was and managed to recruit some pro bono attorney to represent her grandparent's rights. I had already spoken with our family counselor and case worker informing them about the situation. Apparently the dragon queen had also frantically called social services about it and her grandparent's rights. They told her what I already knew. I had full custody of the kids and that I could do what I deemed fit in their best interests. She didn't like what she heard so she found this poor woman who was clearly in above her head to represent her.

At the next family court meeting, before it could begin, my mother and her attorney approached a podium to speak, the judge was very matter of fact with them, professional but firm. The attorney began to speak of grandparents rights and the judge curtly interrupted her. She had already read the reports of my mother and knew what had taken place. She went on to say it was well within my rights to refuse her visitation to the children. Their case had no merit. My mother and her "legal eagle" tucked their tails behind their legs and left the podium but not the court room. I watched as they sat down in the pews like they were going to stick around in hopes of hearing something juicy against us. I remembered that the family courts were closed door sessions. Not open to the public. So I timidly and I mean timidly, raised my hand. Who wants to interrupt a judge? Not me. The judge noticed and was polite in addressing me, I asked her if this was a closed session and she confirmed that; already knowing what I was wondering she asked me if I wanted my mother and her attorney removed from the room and I said " yes mam". It was the most empowering thing for me. It was like standing up to a bully. So the two women were escorted out and then the judge read the reports from our family counselor and social services that were all very good.

Scott was struggling to break free from the meth. But he was determined and kept fighting. Kids were doing great and things were looking up. We continued to see our family counselor and it was the first time ever I was vindicated as she confirmed there is such a thing as psychological and verbal abuse and that I was a survivor of it.

I fight every day to be a survivor. I prefer that term versus victim. I didn't die; victims die… survivors live …. I prefer to live. It was bumpy at times but we were truly blessed to have worked with the people we did on the family court side of things. It was humbling but I needed to be humbled. It was an awakening that gave me some backbone that I needed very much too. Most of all it reminded me of how loving and powerful the Almighty is.   That afternoon when he visited me I was on cloud nine for days. I felt renewed and I told myself I would never forget that feeling of being in his presence.

Sadly, as the years have gone by I have never forgotten what it felt like but I cannot replicate the feeling. It's beyond human comprehension. Better than any high a drug could give. It made me feel complete, content and enlightened. While I have always believed in God to know what it feels like to be in his presence doesn't make me worry about what heaven is like. I just worry about being worthy enough to get there.

FORTY EIGHT

Battling two fronts at once just got easier when our case was dismissed by the family courts. Now we could divert all our attention to the criminal courts and the prosecuting attorney that wanted to send Scott to prison.

Our bulldog attorney taught me a lot of things. Among them was how to play the waiting game. Having to deal with the family courts bought us time because that was primary, considering the welfare of our children was first and foremost. During that time Scott had cleaned up and we took the initiative even before knowing he would face court ordered "classes" dealing with drugs, alcohol and domestic violence. It was kind of a shock to the system that an "offender' was being proactive about the classes and such but he was anxious to keep moving forward and let's face it, it looked good on the reports to the court.

Scotts attorney told us that the longer it takes for a case to go to court the less and less attention would be paid because some other jackass was bound to screw up worse and they would then be the focus of the prosecutions attention. The other thing I learned was that when some officers are on the stand it's not testimony it's a "test-a-lie". Cops have a way of looking at things that aren't necessarily the way it really happened. Case and point was that night I was barraged with the constant intent that I wear out and tell them I was scared for my life. Had I not stood my ground the situation would have been very different. Luckily, my hardheadedness paid off. Nonetheless, there were drugs, guns, booze and domestic violence involved in this affair and it looked bad. The district attorney wanted my husband behind bars… I just wanted him home.

The battle lines my mother drew, I feel, worked in our favor. As hard as she tried to back stab us it only served to discredit her. As we were rebuilding and strengthening our family and learning from the experience we also knew why it all went south as well. Scott and I knew we had to slow things down in our life. We could have bags of money and he could continue to work his ass off but it was all for nothing if we lost sight of what was really important; that was us and our family. If we didn't place the pressure on ourselves then the pressure to do speed to keep going and working in overdrive to achieve lofty means wouldn't be there either.

Originally we looked at buying a house in our beloved Rockies a little mountain town we loved so much. But it meant commuting and long bus rides for the kids. In the end it didn't turn out to offer us any more of a quiet life than we already had.

Christmas 2003, we came back to Missouri to be with Scott's family. It was late the night we got in and as we got closer to Maryville I saw the MFA elevators in the clear winter sky and the moon glowing in the background… It made me ache to come back. I knew then where we needed to be. During our holiday visit I kept my revelation to myself. It wasn't until we had been home for a week or so during a meeting with our family counselor that I brought it up.   It was a no brainer; better life surrounded by Scott's family, in the country, no gangs. The kids didn't know what to think but they didn't object either. When my mother found this out she immediately lobbied the DA's office about how could they allow us to leave and take her grandkids from her. As part of full disclosure I was given copies of her letters and statements made by my friend whose place I stayed the night of what I term the "great train wreck". Several years back as part of letting it go and forgiving my mother, yet again, I burnt those letters and that whole file of the court case I felt it was time to move on so in the bon fire they went. How gullible I was to think she could never top that betrayal.

We continued to cooperate and work with the court system. Reports from Scott's classes were all good. Our family court file was available to the criminal judge and the fact that we weren't high risk on their scale; actually we were the lowest risk, all of that played in our favor. The day came for us to finally go to court. We were well armed with the truth and God on our side. The District Attorney put me on the stand. His last name sounded more like pew but was spelled more like puke. And I let it slip when I addressed him as Mr. Puke on purpose. I couldn't resist. The man was out to get my husband; I wasn't going to have any of it. He was polite when correcting me but it took me a couple times to finally get his name right.

It was obvious from our file case and all the documentation on Scott that he wasn't a bad guy he just got caught up on bad things and it got the better of him. He didn't deserve to go to prison. When I was asked on the stand how I would describe Scott's progress I referred to it as a metamorphosis. The judge commented that even he didn't know what the word meant. I couldn't believe that. But I cut him some slack. After all, he was the one guy I didn't want to screw with. At all times Scott and I never once appeared at a court preceding not looking professional and at all times we behaved as the people we were with integrity and honor and honesty. It served us well and after all of it was over Scott managed to avoid prison and we moved our family to Missouri.

FORTY NINE

It was the beginning of 2004 and everything was starting to come together for us. Scott had a line on a job with a great company in Maryville. It was tax time and I wanted to work with my old employer for the last time so my days were filled with kids my job at school and the nights were spent working for a well known tax preparation company. It was during one of those nights that the judge that presided over the criminal court case came in to get his taxes done. I happened to be at the front desk when he paid his bill. I introduced myself saying I knew he probably didn't remember me but that I wanted to personally thank him for being fair and just. As I stood up to shake his hand I could see the look of shock in his face. It was understandable that he wouldn't know how to react as I doubt this occasion has ever happened to him. We made some small talk and he left with a smile I was grateful for the opportunity.

Scott was offered the job in Maryville and needed to be there before school let out for the summer. That meant six weeks apart but we had no choice. The kids and I stayed behind to finish the school year. Memorial weekend came and Scott flew back to help me finish packing. We loaded up our truck, a moving van and my brother–in- laws big rig and headed to Missouri.

It was very difficult to leave my dearest friend as I know the uncertainty and leaving their friends was hard for the kids as well. I was convinced this move was what was for the best. I knew it would have its ups and downs but I just knew it was for the best. I allowed my mother to see the kids for the last time, with the good byes said and the house locked up our little caravan set off across I- 80 headed to a new beginning.

It took me a long time to recover from my mother's betrayal. In time we slowly reunited. I don't know if it's because I am truly weak or if family means so much to me that I would suck up anything. My boys wanted little to do with my mother however; Katy was still young and very much attached to her. I don't know how much is too much but I figured if I could forgive Scott than I should forgive her so I did. I realize now years later how ridiculous the comparison was, the stark contrast between the two. Scott never once shied away from the fact that he made some huge mistakes and was responsible for some of the hardships we survived. My mother lived in denial as to the part she played. Scott took inventory of his life and knew he wanted better. He wanted to be better not just for the kids or me but he had to be better for himself. My mother was not the same in any regard.

After all the years of enduring and shaking off behaviors and attitudes from my mother it was empowering to have the understanding, recognition and acknowledgement that in fact my mother was an abuser. The source of the recognition was rather surprising as it would have been the last thing I would ever have imagined to come up from the legal situation we had to go through. She showed her true colors to people outside of the family, they knew her for what she was and it was the first time I felt relieved that what I felt she did was abuse was truly that and that I wasn't nuts thinking it was.

For the first time in my life I could finally say I knew what it was like to feel that my soul was at peace. Scott was doing great, better and better with each day. I had to learn to let my guard down and to not be on the defense as I had always had to be before. Never knowing what to expect around Scott and most days just walking on egg shells around him, things were different now and I was getting to know Scott all over again in many ways.

 We weren't without casualties in the move. It was difficult on the kids but I had faith it was for the best. We lost our house to foreclosure as the market was in the pooper at the time we moved. Although we knew we would each take a 40 percent reduction in annual wages by moving to Missouri; we still clung to hope that we could pay off our debt but ended up filing bankruptcy. It was the only move for us, without it we were condemned to financial purgatory. Rather humiliating but nonetheless a necessity to our future. We now had a simple life and I have never looked back. To feel for the first time in my life that my soul was at peace was everything to me. Our family shared many wonderful times some of them including my mother. It is this that makes her final betrayal even harder to deal with. I welcomed her back into our lives despite the degradation and belittlement she was guilty of so deftly dispensing to my children.

FIFTY

As I write this I feel like I am the betrayer of memories. I wished I could say that despite all the bad there were still some good memories but I can't say it. And I would be lying if I told you there weren't any good memories. This woman brought such contradiction into my life. I spent my whole life just surviving, constantly in a hurry to get somewhere but I didn't know where. I just knew it wasn't where I was at that moment. Dealing with the instability of her personality was a full time job. I don't remember times when I was nurtured or cuddled or even being told growing up that she was proud of me. I want to believe they happened but I can't say they did. I kept being molested by a man I thought was my grandfather ,a secret so my life wouldn't get any shittier and it would keep people I didn't trust out of my life. We three kids never had a chance to have a good sibling relationship, we were so busy trying to survive that we had no time for each other. As a very young child I dreamed for years of marrying a man and being his wife forever and having a family. My immediate dream was to get to where I was old enough to go live with my dad. I dreamed of being 16 and moving out, I dreamed of being on my own and being free. Free from her, from the past, from the tension I lived with, free from the oppression. This was all I knew. It was my normal.

Unlike it seems to be for many kids today, school was just a part of my life that I knew had to be completed. I didn't calculate how many F's I could get and still graduate. I didn't bring my home and private drama with me to school nor did I make my problems part of my social scene. I was an average student that had a few friends and never participated in sports or clubs. Flunking a class or even getting a D grade was not an option for me and although I could have easily gotten straight A's that wasn't on my radar either. I was content being a B-C student doing my work and getting by. For the most part I was a loner because my self-esteem and body image kept me that way.

I fought being overweight my whole life. One time in kindergarten our class had to line up and be weighed in front of each other. I was the chubbiest kid in class and weighed in at over 90 pounds. I was also the tallest kid but the pounds per inch of height couldn't hide the fact I was morbidly obese. I got used to seeing that nasty label all the time especially when I would go to the doctor.

What few friends I had could be called the refuse of the class along with myself. We weren't the pretty ones; we didn't wear the high dollar name brand clothing. We weren't superficial either. Despite our lack of popularity we still had good times and it made school not suck so bad.

By the time I was 13, I was smoking cigarettes. It wasn't hard to hide from my mother; she smoked as well and didn't miss the occasional cigarette or notice the smell on me since I lived in a home with a smoker that much hadn't changed. After turning 14, I went to a party with my first official boyfriend and was introduced to pot. I wasn't impressed; all it did was give me a bad headache. Thankfully the beer I was drinking took care of the headache.

I wasn't a problem child. I was the child that slipped through all the cracks. We loved to cruise downtown Fort Collins and my only claim to being any sort of rebel is getting a ticket for loitering with my boyfriend. He came from a well to do family.

I was like the girl from the other side of the tracks for him. He was almost two years older than me and had a car that looked like what Starsky and Hutch drove in the TV show. Old town Fort Collins happened to be a great place to cruise however, the business patrons in the area didn't care much for our presence. Overall we didn't cause any problems other than traffic was a little slower as we cruised and parking was a little more difficult. It was how we stayed out of trouble on Friday and Saturday nights. In the summer we added Wednesday night to the lineup.

Eventually, it was blown out of proportion by the police department and they started issuing loitering tickets. On the night in question I was out with my boyfriend cruising but it wasn't were I told my mother I was at. In my defense it was a last minute thing and the opportunity was too good to pass up. So we are all downtown and we pullover and park because we were going to ride with some of our other friends in their car. This officer watched us park and get out and head over to the other vehicle but stops us midway. The jack ass gave us both a fifteen dollar loitering ticket. I was horrified, that was the end of my life as I knew it. I'd never been in trouble like that before and I just knew my mother was going to tan my hide if she found out. My boyfriend paid the fines a month later but not before I lived in morbid fear that there would be some letter or something sent to her since I was a juvenile. None ever came thankfully.

Cruising was such a hot topic at that time because of the issues downtown and how us kids felt we were getting the shaft. It ended up being a topic of discussion in my Civics class. Actually it became a debate of which the outcome was that if I wrote a letter to the local paper called the Fort Collins Triangle and it got published that I would get an A in the class for the term. Challenge accepted! So I wrote the letter addressing our side of the matter, my teacher sent it in and a week later I got an A.

The one thing I hadn't counted on was if my mother would see it in the paper. She never did. I still have the clipping in my scrapbook. I was in my early twenties before I told her about it.

You would never guess by looking at me what I was really all about. The one obvious result of this was that I was always way more mature than my peers. I had to be.

FIFTY ONE

As I entered the preteen years my mother and I knocked heads more frequently. I hated her more than I loved her. I knew she worked hard to provide for us but she was vacant when it came to providing unconditional, all accepting love. If you didn't see things her way it was wrong. Not only were you wrong you were also ill and needed help from the twisted reality you lived in. There was never any compromise with her.

My brother had moved out years before and it wasn't without its fall out. It was the summer; Brad was 15 years old and was given the opportunity to work on a relative's ranch in Wyoming. It was an awesome chance for him to just be a cowboy and work as a ranch hand. Something he very much wanted to do. Our mother had agreed to it with the understanding that he come home two weeks prior to school so that he could get ready for the new year. It was a fun summer as I got to visit him with our father and sometimes my mom and I would go up. It was always more fun with my dad because he would either bring our mini bikes or the amphibious six-wheeler. The ranch was huge so often times we would take our rifles and spend the afternoon shooting prairie dogs.

 Aside from the cattle, horses and of course the prairie dogs that lived in abundance in the prairie lands were rattlesnakes. My cousins would shoot them and skin them and hang the hides on the clothes line to dry out. At any given time I would see no less than 5 or 10 hides drying either on the fence or clothesline. That's just the ones that came close to the house.

In the kitchen they had a bowl and large jars filled with rattlers from the snakes they had killed. Some small many of them rather large, none of them I liked to be near to. I hate snakes they scare the hell out of me.

Summer came to an end and school was fast approaching. It was time for Brad to come home. He loved it were he was and just wanted to spend one more week there. It was absolutely out of the question for my mother. It really wasn't a big deal but to my mother it was, most likely more because it wasn't her way, never the compromiser. The whole issue got out of control fast and thus started what would resemble the Hatfield's and McCoy's. Albeit an earlier agreement was being broken, but it wasn't worth the outfall, all the damage, that took place if she would have just compromised.

 She took a sheriff's deputy to the ranch to retrieve my brother from there it got nastier. My brother had already had his fill of her, all the years of verbal badgering and hollering. He definitely didn't want to go home with her now. Brad wanted to live with our father something I wanted so badly myself. He was at the age he could speak for himself and so he did. Our mother wouldn't relent and from then on our lives would take another twist for the worse.

We were dragged in and out and thru the court system all because she couldn't compromise. Over the next few years that's all I would know. In the end the only people that came out of that experience unscathed where the attorneys' and their fat billfolds. It was such a mangled mess of manipulation and hurt.

My brother ended up staying in a halfway house for delinquents because he refused to go home to her. When all she had to do was allow him to live with our father. But that would mean compromise and ultimately not getting her way. Even at our expense she would still be this way. It must have been horrific for my brother. Brad was never a problem child his only crime was he didn't want to return home to her. Because she had full custody and wouldn't allow him to live with our father he was put away. So much for a court system that was meant to protect kids, they didn't do shit for us!

Eventually my brother was able to get out of that nasty place and did end up being able to live with Bert. For the longest time the only way I could see my brother after that was when he would come to my school and get me out of class. We would spend the few minutes we had in the hall; it was always emotional for me. I loved seeing my big brother. Sometimes he would pick me up from school and drive me within a block of our house and then I would have to walk the rest of the way. These visits were our secret for a long time. Once my mother found out about them she went through the roof and called the principal. That was the end of our visits at school. My brother was my hero, he may not have lived at home anymore but he didn't leave me behind.

I only know what I witnessed, my brother and I have never really spoke about that time. It was the crux of my hurt and the catalyst for my desire to leave her the first chance I could get.

FIFTY TWO

Our mother was always convinced that our dad bad mouthed her when we would be with him. Our grandma Hilzer would only say that she could forgive but could never forget. Our mother on the other hand was never short on words to put our dad down. She never acknowledged our pleading for her to quit, it was all about making herself feel better at our expense.

By the time I was nearing 15 our fights became more frequent. Her unvoiced expectations that I was meant to telepathically read and carry out were a huge issue. It was impossible to read her mind so we fought a lot. Infrequently they would become physical. More times it was just a slap. Often I was able to deflect them and return the favor. I hated her. I wasn't a bad child. I kept my room clean I did chores when she asked me to do them. Our arguments were over attitudes mostly. She would say I had a bad attitude. This may have been true however; my attitude was a defensive one from experiencing her venomous tongue and attitude first. I did the best I could to avoid her and spent most of my childhood in my room or outside.

As a teenager I was in my room all the time just to keep the peace. She would start a fight over that and when I would tell her why I spend so much time in my room she would deny there was any problem and that it was all me. I was sick and needed help. Funny, I didn't feel the need to stay in my room when I was staying with my dad. On the contrary, I couldn't get enough of him and his hugs. I couldn't do enough for him.

Sometimes our fights would end with me calling my dad begging to come live with him. At some point in the argument I would bring it up and she would say call your dad go ahead. I'd call him begging him to let me come live with him crying and sobbing that it was too much then she would take the phone from my hands and tell him that I was being belligerent and in denial and needed help. These phone calls never ended without her screaming at him as well. I was trapped; I had been trapped since I was very little.

I was counting the days, with my upcoming 16th birthday also came my chance to run and that's exactly what I was going to do. Anyone with any sense would have seen the writing on the wall, except for my mother. I hardly doubt she was naive. She was most definitely in denial. To not see the writing on the wall and at least sense that once I got my own wheels that I was going to bolt was just plain stupid.

My father bought me a nice little Toyota Celica. The only thing about it was that it was a five speed. I didn't know how to drive a stick. It was parked at my brother's place waiting for me. By this time being five years older than me Brad was now 21 and on his own.

The day I got my license I went over and got my car and found that the best gear I could run in was reverse. It was a hard knocks education for me. I did have a little drive time with the car but I was a terrible manual transmission driver. I can't count the stoplights and stop signs I either stalled the motor or almost rolled back into the car behind me.

One thing my mother and I have in common is that both our birthdays are in February. For that whole month things were pretty quiet. When March rolled around the smoke signals were in the air and not long after she was on the warpath. I don't remember what we fought over but I do remember that she tried to take my car away. That wasn't going to happen. She didn't own it. It was in my name. Nor did she insure it or pay for the gas in it, my father did. The argument escalated as they all do with her. There never is such a thing as just talking with her and she is always the first to raise her voice nothing ever ends well when this happens; that night was no different. She challenged me again to call my father so I did. The difference with this phone call was that I just said I was packing my things and coming to stay with him. She grabbed the phone and hung up. There were words exchanged and I went to my room.

It was a Thursday night and I had enough. It was true I was waiting for the opportunity to leave. I didn't hasten the chance I just waited. I knew she would lose it and she did. Four a.m. the next morning I was up and getting ready for school, packing everything I thought I was going to need and I quietly loaded my car. I left early that morning for school so as to not have any further interactions with her. I never went back.

Leaving Mandy there alone with her was hard. I wanted to take my little sister with me but it was impossible. To this day I feel guilty about leaving her. We were to never have that sisterly bond, that relationship where we even really know each other. She was eight years old when I left. I missed out on a lot but I was so damn miserable living with our mother I had to leave. After I left the house that morning I felt a small sliver of freedom was on my horizon. I knew my life would change a lot. I fully expected her to put up a fight for me to be returned like she did for my brother. I truly hoped she would leave me alone and for the most part she did. She was flat broke from the last go around that was probably my saving grace. She did try to lobby me and persuade me to return but I wasn't having any of it. As a matter of fact I wanted nothing to do with her.

FIFTY THREE

I was still a smoker; I did a little pot and a little speed. Mostly cross tops and black beauties. I knew a guy that was training to be an EMT and he always had a line on something and always shared it with me. Drugs and alcohol where just things to do for me, I didn't need them. Looking back I think at that time it was just the thrill of doing it. Bert had taken every opportunity to teach my brother and I that drugs were a crutch for life and that life was worth living. We hung on every word he said. Even knowing this I still did drugs it was kind of like rebelling and doing what I want because I wasn't supposed to. I wasn't hooked and looking for where I was going to get my next high. I whole heartedly agreed with what Bert told us and to this day I believe it was his "preaching" that is the reason for any strength I had to not suffer through addiction. I just wanted to live life and experience everything. I wanted to be free and just breathe without the thought that I was going to get yelled at.

I had a boyfriend at that time that was 7years older than me. My mother didn't like that. I didn't blame her. I could understand that part. While she had threatened to make me break up with him, which there was no way in hell that was going to happen, he wasn't the reason for why I left. He was, however, the reason for why I didn't end up dead on the interstate from driving drunk or worse.

He may have been 7 years my senior but for over 2 years he kept me out of trouble and taught me a few things in the process. I needed a place to land and I found one with him. In exchange for the dope I still drank a little. When I managed to get shit faced he made sure my car keys were nowhere to be found.

Instead of hanging with the hard core partiers we hung out with farm kids. Our idea of a good time was farming all night long. And all day long. We had a fairly new John Deer and an old Caterpillar we called Queenie. More often than not I got Queenie but didn't care. My boyfriend taught me how to run a tractor and I loved it. Together we would mulch, disc, plow you name it all night long and most of our weekends where spent farming.

For the time I was with my "farm boy" if I wasn't at school I was farming with him. I was still living with my dad but only during the weekdays on occasion would he see me. I was doing well. I was staying out of trouble, I was happy and I was FREE.

FIFTY FOUR

My father lived in Greeley and at the time I ran away from my mother she was living outside Ft. Collins Colorado with her fourth husband. I finished my sophomore year driving every day from Greeley to Ft. Collins to go to school. My junior year I transferred to Greeley West in Greeley. My dad and I had a great life. I was so thankful for him, I never stopped being thankful.

I guess it was unpreventable that we should grow apart. After all, my "farm boy" was much older than me. I had started a new school and was making new friends. Being chubby wasn't acceptable to me and so I bought some diet pills that are no longer on the market but worked wondrously for me, I lost a bunch of weight and got a hot body.

Up until then I was wearing 36x34 wranglers and doing everything but having them painted on just to wear them. Laying on the bed and sucking in my gut I would scale the skin on my fingers just trying to get them zipped and buttoned.

I never was one for weighing myself. I hated scales ever since kindergarten. As I lost weight I just got a belt and then when the belt wasn't enough I would get my sewing machine out and take my jeans in by sewing the side seams. Once those options were exhausted then I went to buy new jeans.

The greatest day of my teenage life was when I went to the Buckle to buy some Levis and I tried on the 34'sfirst, they were too big. Then I tried on the 32 waist 501's and they were too big. Finally the sales gal says let me help you and so she brought me a pair of jeans I just slipped on and they were still a little loose. I stepped out of the fitting room and looked in the mirror. I looked fabulous, even had a cute butt, who knew. I asked her what size they were she replied "29x 34". I was shocked I had no idea I had lost that much weight. I didn't even take the jeans off. I paid for them and proudly wore them home.

Getting older and now with a skinny body I wanted other things from life. I had been living a good life before, staying out of trouble, had a lot of fun farming, but I wanted to live life I wanted the adventure and my boyfriend who I was now promised to was ready to settle down and didn't care about doing all those things. So I gave him back his ring and stepped into the single life.

I didn't stay single for long the short time I was single sucked terribly. Losing a bunch of weight hadn't changed who I hung with. I didn't venture over to the "other side". There weren't any farmers at Greeley West; we were considered the country club high school. My friends were all the misfits that hung together. Many of them kids like me, just trying to survive their life. I met a young man who would be a part of my life for the next six months. We had some really great times, spent our weekends partying mainly drinking and of course I stayed with him a lot as he had his own place at 18. It was never meant to be. I never really saw us making a life together.

FIFTY FIVE

The night I would meet Scott I wasn't looking for anyone or anything in particular. The bar was a fun place to go and cut loose. The people there didn't know me from Adam. I wasn't the used to be fat kid or the loner from school. Here it was a fresh start. I was a cute little blonde chick and so the fun began. When I first met Scott I wasn't all that taken with him. He seemed aloof and unapproachable. He was always with a wild and crazy friend of his and so with them two and my friend and me and anyone else that drank with us we would party. The second time we met was different we got a long a little better but he still seemed distant. I was just looking to have some fun not really wanting a relationship. Somehow fate maneuvered circumstances and we ended up going on a date.

Our first official date started out going for a steak at a ritzy place in town only to get there and find out their kitchen closed for the night so we ended up at a Denny's. Scott had a big truck that he had just bought and it was hard for me to get in and out of it but it was a nice truck, that was points in his favor despite ending up eating at Denny's.

I don't know if anything would have come out of that date if it hadn't been for the fact that I remembered his last name. A few days later I had to put my car in the shop. And I needed a ride home from school. So the night before I looked in the phone book and found a number that eventually was the right one to get a hold of him at. He said he'd pick me up and the next day he zoomed in the school parking lot on a motorcycle and gave me a ride home. If my car wouldn't have been put in the shop and I needed a ride home to this day I wonder if we would have ever dated.

 After all these years I look back at the events and how things played out and despite all the hardships I am convinced that we were brought together by a higher power and that if we had been paired with anyone else the relationship would not have lasted. God gave us each other because no one else was tough enough for us both.

Scott was always the gentlemen we had gone on numerous dates before our relationship went any further, but after that we were inseparable.   I didn't know what the hell a pipeliner was yet, but he was one I also knew he would have to travel. We hadn't been dating long before he had to leave for a job in northeastern Colorado.

Scott and I partied a lot, I could drink and had no problem holding my own when it came to that. Scott and his friends liked to party harder than that but I didn't care. There was something about this guy that I was attracted to. He was kind of mysterious and definitely cute. What he saw in me I have no clue but I was glad he saw something. I liked being his girl. I liked being known as his girlfriend. It really sucked when he had to go out of town on that job.

FIFTY SIX

Scott hadn't been gone long just about a week and I get a phone call, he's in jail in some podunker little town and needed bailed out. I was just the gal to do that. I never once gave it a second thought. Like maybe this isn't what I was looking for in a boyfriend or this isn't the kind of thing I want to be a part of. None of that crossed my mind for one minute.

I had met his parents in a rather unconventional way, we had gone to the bar and needed a place to crash so we came back to his parents' house and pulled out their sleeper sofa and passed out. Early that morning his father got up to go take a shower and walked through the living room in his underwear. I met his mother a short time after that sitting at their kitchen table. It was like nothing out of the ordinary that I was there. Scott hadn't ever brought a girl home before. His mother was so sweet and cordial about it.

Going to where she worked and telling her that Scott was in jail wasn't all that difficult for me. Seeing her breakdown in tears over it was tough. We hadn't known each other but days. I had only seen her once before and there I was hugging her and telling her it would be ok. I called in to school and told my guidance counselor I wouldn't be there and then along with one of Scott's little brothers we set off to bust him out jail.

Starting out we were under the impression that he got a DWAI or driving while ability impaired. Once we got to our destination it become something more. From the time they jailed Scott for the DWAI and we got there the maid at his hotel found a brown bag full of what was thought to be marijuana. Scott's bail went from 300 to 3000 dollars. Walking in to the jailhouse with the initial 300 dollars and ready to bail Scott out; the kindly Sherriff took me and his brother into his office and told us they had found the pot in his room under the bed. And so it was a $3000 bail. I acted all shocked even though I was and I wasn't. The smart ass in me wanted to ask the sheriff if now that they knew he had it, if I could have it back. I knew Scott smoked but had no idea he had that much on him. So we were allowed to see him for a few minutes then we went and made the call to his mom, we needed 3000 bucks instead.

 Scott had that much in his account and so it was just a matter of getting it wired to us. We spent the time waiting for the money by going and getting his truck out of impound and then getting a bite to eat at a local burger joint. We got his truck back in a mess. It was obvious that the local PD tore it up looking for more drugs. We had Thor, the viscous pit bull (NOT) with us and so here was this demon dog in my car watching us eat a burger at a local diner while the townspeople watched us and Thor as they speculated about why we were there and if we were part of some big syndicated drug ring. The news of Scotts capture was already known throughout town. It was obvious we could feel their eyes burning holes in our backs. The money came and we liberated Scott from jail and headed home.

30 days later we returned to "smallville" for court. I was nervous. Scott never hired an attorney and so we didn't know how it was going to go down. He was thinking jail time but I was naive and really pretty ignorant as this was my first experience of this nature. We sat in the court room for what seemed to be forever; finally they call Scott's case. He goes up

and talks to the judge and the prosecuting attorney. I can't hear what's going on real well but I see heads shaking and some shuffling around. Apparently the evidence, said to be 4-5 pounds of "definite Cannabis Sativa L", we never figured out what the L was for, had disappeared.

 The judge was fit to be tied. With no evidence how was he going to rule on the case. The sheriff had run out of time to provide the bag of pot and so Scott got off with a DWAI and the money we spent on bail was retained as court costs and fines. Scott had to take some classes and there were some other miniscule things he had to complete like community service but all in all he fared better than he would have had that bag of pot been found.

Reveling in our day's success we drove back to Greeley and since it was kind of late we checked into a motel. Neither one of us wanted to go home so we went to Motel Eight instead. Glad the day was over we both smoked a joint while lying in bed and watching TV. It was around 9:30 p.m. I remember the time and the TV show we were watching. It was Hotel, a series with James Brolin in it. As we were decompressing some red lights peek through the curtains. Red lights like on the top of a tow truck.

"Scott, you should see what that is"

He says, "You get up and see what it is."

"Naw, I aint getting up."

The next morning we both got up and the truck was gone. A brand new 1985 Dodge Ram 4x4 truck had vanished. A beautiful black truck with gold pin striping that was stolen right from under our noses. Scott hadn't had it long enough to make the first payment. And the dog he bought to guard it slept on the floor near his master and his girlfriend as it happened. We were too stoned to get up the night before to check out the flashing lights. Being stoned may have been a curse or a blessing that night. Had one of us got up and con-fronted the car thief who's to say we wouldn't have been shot over the deal. In the end the truck was fully insured. We got robbed but Scott got his money back. From my point of view what was even sadder was instead of going to Prom in his cool truck he was now going to take me to prom in a shitty faded baby blue rental car.

FIFTY SEVEN

There is no doubt our life together has been full. It definitely has not been what you could define as usual or normal by any stretch. Unconventional, crazy wild, completely dysfunctional and successful would be more like it. I think I would have been bored with any other life. I've always loved a good challenge my life and marriage has certainly been full of them. Closing in on 50 now I feel like the wind has been let out of my sails. For very brief moments that I can count on one hand for the last 47 years have I ever felt like my soul was at peace.

These past years have finally taken their toll. It's very hard for me not to feel like I have struggled enough and wonder why it is that I can't catch a break in life and experience more moments of peace. Then I watch the news or read something on the internet and I feel like a spoiled whiny child. There is always someone out there who has it way worse than I. Yet I can't help but pray and hope and dream for things to be better.

Nowadays I really do feel like that cartoon guy the born loser. Now that my children are grown it's painful and gut wrenching to watch them make their own way in life. Despite trying to give them the best start I could I really do believe that I have failed them. All three graduated from high school and both my sons got a great start in college but it was short lived.

My oldest son, Zac, joined the Missouri National Guard when he was 17 and had a full ride to college. He deployed to Afghanistan, turned 21 overseas and came home to us a changed man. I think he struggles with so much just surviving as a single guy is hard. He now works in security and has to keep a second job just to make ends meet. At 24, he is still a young man I pray so hard that doors open for him and that he will find that perfect woman that compliments him and together they complete each other.

My middle son, Jake, at 23 has such talent , while both my sons area great writers Jake also has a comedic timing and a sense of humor that just makes you roll on the floor laughing till your sides hurt. He would be a great radio personality. It would have to be satellite radio because the fines for his language could be excessive. The list grows of the things Jake hasn't found to be his forte, with each one I like to think we are one experience closer to him figuring out what it is he will do career wise. With Jakes recent move back to Colorado I think he is well on his way towards that goal.

Together my boys are quite the duo as a matter of fact Scott would always call them the Dynamic Duo. There is nothing they wouldn't do for each other or for their little sister. We raised them, teaching them that no matter what the world may throw at them they would always have each other. They were Cronk tough. Alone they are strong but together they are stronger. If I had to say there was one thing I did right, that would be it.

It is so very hard to watch my kid's struggle, so I pray. I pray at night, in the car as I drive to work and home, I pray constantly. It's comforting to know that when I or their dad can't be there for them, that they have each other.

The path our daughter Haley Katherine, or Katy as we call her, took started out to be impressive and promising. She graduated from high school early, barley over 17 and started college a couple months later. Before finishing her first semester she decided to enlist with the Missouri National Guard. I can't say we were totally surprised. Katy has always been competitive and loves to do one better than her brothers. It makes the end result that much more heartbreaking.

It was a huge family event when Scott and I signed Katy's enlistment papers. On a weekend home from college Katy brought the documents up with her. It worked out great that any NCO or non commissioned officer could witness our signatures. Sgt. Zac Cronk was an NCO, so on Katy's papers there is nothing but a bunch of Cronk signatures. Naturally we took pictures; it was a big deal and a moment of great pride for all involved.

Katy did her Basic training at Ft Leonard Wood and again her graduation was as big a deal as her brother's was at Ft. Jackson. We all attended and spent every minute we could with her before she had to leave for Ft. Lee to do her AIT. She turned 18 in Virginia at Ft. Lee. She graduated and came home. It was not long after coming home she was told her battalion was deploying. Having gone through that with Zac we tried to be excited but it was hampered with a lot of weariness. We were lucky our son came home to us. But he had a hard time adjusting. Would we be lucky one more time? While the deployments were different they each had their own set of very real dangers.

We had no idea the biggest danger of all was lurking among her battalion. Katy spent months pre-mobilizing in Idaho and finally at Ft. Hood Texas.

In May of 2013 she had to have her wisdom teeth pulled. While alone recovering from the procedure in her barracks she was sexually assaulted by an individual in her command. Under the influence of pain medication and alone this animal stole something from my daughter that she will never recover from. This was a man she looked up to, thought of him as a mentor and spent as much time as she could learning from him and he took advantage of her condition and raped her body, her soul and her spirit.

 Her battalion command was inexperienced and not properly trained in my opinion, between that and the burden of inefficiency our military operates so deftly under, combined it would all lead to what has been termed as a "Total Failure" by the military. What I call it is gross negligence. The incident did not involve just my daughter but at least several other young women. Given the circumstances of Katy's assault she didn't report it immediately. It wasn't until literally 24 hours before she was to deploy that the matter was brought to light. Yet she chose to stay with her battalion and deploy thinking she would be taken care of.

In the following months Katy broke up with her boyfriend, became very solemn, depressed and refused to talk about the assault. As her parents, we didn't want to make things worse for her and so we tried to be supportive and encouraging thinking all the while that things were being done to help her and it was just slow getting to her. This was not the case. By October of 2013 my level of concern was sky high. Katy was crying in private and at work, she was back and forth in her relationships. Her behavior and emotions where not normal for the Katy we knew and raised. It was obvious as her parents we had to step in.

FIFTY EIGHT

At first I emailed her command that in turn turned out to be a total waste of time. One of them of went straight to her to tell her we were inquiring about her. Which I didn't particularly mind but felt it was underhanded. I wasn't going to hide the communication from her I needed information before I approached her about it. The insensitivity and juvenile thoughtlessness exhibited by certain individuals towards Katy was inexcusable. Case and point, Katy had stopped eating, at one point she passed out at bus stop on base and had to go to the camp hospital. ALL the signs were clearly there a kindergartner could have read them or someone who really cared or even those individuals who were supposedly trained on this or what was called the SHARP Team in her unit. But none did, she fell through the cracks of a system full of failures. On one occasion a woman who was Katy's superior on the job cracked a comment that if she didn't eat all her babies would be born deformed. It put Katy in tears and it cemented the fact that no one was there for her that should have been.

Shortly after Katy's arrival in Afghanistan she and the other girls were interrogated by what is called the CID, criminal investigators. It was to be a questioning but Katy was interrogated and manhandled by these individuals who as part of their job were trained to be listeners and to handle victims more humanly yet they chose to not follow that training and the abrasiveness of that interaction set a poor tone with Katy. They confronted her at work and in public none of the interactions were with the due and proper respect owed a victim. It was agonizing. Never before in my life did I feel such agony. I was empty and felt lost. Then I got mad then I started shaking trees and jerking chains. I emailed the sexual assault contact on Military One Source. Military One Source is an awesome website that has been the most beneficial to me through both deployments I am grateful they were there when I needed them. At first while they were sympathetic about the deal there seemed to be a little finger pointing about why no one knew about my daughter and her situation half way across the planet. It had something to do with how the assault was initially reported which I wasted no time pointing out that it didn't matter she was still in crisis and she as well as the other victims should have been followed up on to see how they were doing and they weren't. The truth was that Katy was never given an option as to how the rape was reported. Sure they got interrogated but did anyone from victim's advocacy give a crap to see how the girls were...NO! From this point forward a series of missteps slowly began to become apparent.

My daughter was slipping away from us and I couldn't reach out to her and be there for her and the people that where there with her weren't doing a damn thing that needed to be done. I was eventually hooked up with two state level soldiers who worked the victim's advocacy in Missouri and they were of some help but Katy's biggest problem was those around her and their lack of training and for some, professionalism as well. At one point her command actually told my state level guy that Katy had met with an advocate, when I asked Katy if finally after all the months of emails and phone calls she had got a victims advocate assigned to her, she said NO. Her command had flat out lied to the state. Katy was never assigned an advocate in Afghanistan. When my daughter was recovering from her episode of passing out at the bus stop, she was left alone for the three days she was ordered on bed rest. Her command did not check on her, no one was there. My 18 year old daughter was deep in the depths of depression and dealing with the assault all text book behavior, and no one was there. At one point when she felt she was at one of her lowest times, afraid that she would do something to hurt herself and scared to be alone. It was when she was alone in her barracks that the assault happened. Katy sought out the one person that, despite all the roller coaster of emotions and words and such that victims go through, had always tried to be there for her even when she was pushing people away, her boyfriend. Because she sought safety in going to him and his barracks they both were given an article 15. While against military regulations this is a matter that would not have occurred had Katy not fell through the cracks and been ignored by her command. Yet that same command saw fit to level and article 15 against them both. Katy lost a whole month's wages over that and it was completely unjust and as such is a matter being pursued for expulsion from her record as well as reinstatement of the wages lost. I believe to this day that had Katy not sought out support from the only person she could trust that she very well could have come home to me in a body bag...to receive an article 15 is ludicrous.

The folly of falling short on the military's part continues to this day. Katy was the youngest soldier in her battalion she was to have a part in the coming home ceremony. She couldn't bring herself to be a part of the sham. There were some soldiers close to her that tried to be supportive but none really knew the extent of how Katy suffered while deployed. So it would be unfair to generalize any shortcomings on the soldiers she served with who did their job bravely, competently and with integrity. For Katy coming home didn't involve a huge ceremony it was delayed plane ride, two days prior to her battalions arrival, late at night into Kansas City International

Airport where her mother and big brother were the only ones that could be there to welcome her home. Getting to that point was a whole other battle.

Katy survived deployment and as demobilization came to the forefront the fact that the battalion was coming home via Ft. Hood was a serious problem. She was told by a care giver that they would be able to give her a prescription to help with the anxiety. The military is so good at involving more people than is necessary in a simple matter as a result this never happened. By the time the paperwork and process was followed it was too close to her leaving Afghanistan for them to prescribe anything for her. Her anxiety went through the roof, her sleeplessness was off the charts and she was a bigger mess. Almost home yet so far, she was constantly in tears and did not want to demobilize via Fort Hood as that was where the assault happened and where her assailant was still at. Because I'm not sure I can say this scumbag piece of shits name and because I would take more pleasure in referring to him as the piece of shit than you would like to read about, I will call him "Captain". Despite being stripped of his command Captain was detained at Ft. Hood all through the deployment. He is on duty and getting paid still to this day. We are arguing with Tricare insurance just to get Katy's doctor bills paid and still being billed co-payments for her hospital and doctor visits, but this shit bag is still on duty and getting paid. Is it me or is something wrong here? I lobbied with the battalion commander arguing that Katy should not go through Ft. Hood but it was overruled and so she had no choice.

From the moment she landed till the moment I could fly her out she was nothing but a ball of nerves. With some more chain jerking she was quickly and finally assigned an advocate at Ft. Hood who turned out to be a blessing. Her command at this point were nothing but apologetic to Katy once they were questioned by the Ft. Hood advocate people but it was too little too late. Damage was already done. Their sincerity was questionable and I view it as a total cover your ass move. Katy wanted nothing to do with them she wanted to be home. For the few days she was at Hood she had little comfort in knowing there was a no contact order placed on Captain. He couldn't be anywhere near where she was at. If she was going in a building that he was at he had to leave.

It was harrowing for her always wondering if he was somewhere watching her or if this restraining order was really going to keep him from getting to her. After all he knew a lot of people. It was evident during deployment that there were individuals who were loyal to him. He didn't have to be there or near her to know what was going on.

I can't fully describe the heartache I felt. My arms physically hurt to hold my little girl again. We were on the phone constantly and had it not been for her advocate at Ft. Hood things would have been very different. The anxiety was too much despite the support she was now getting. She wanted to be home. I was at the end of my rope and made a few calls and even went so far as to begin arrangements to pay for Katy's flight home if they would just get her to the plane. I had enough of the military and its bullshit... finally they agreed to get her on a plane and so she was flown home. It was February just before my birthday, she was home alive and in my arms. It was the best birthday present ever, but a long hard fought one.

FIFTY NINE

You'd think it ends here but it doesn't. Katy was home but she wasn't the Katy we knew. Her spirit is broken her esteem is gone. She no longer had the foundation in her life for her future that her military career once served as. My war was now on three fronts. First and foremost to see that Katy receives everything that is owed to her. Second to see that the bag of shit gets court-martialed with what I am told is 4 pages of charges and still growing. Third to see that the United States Government addresses this issue and that when it comes to sexual assault training that giggling adults and snickering boys in the back row, like it's a junior high school class, isn't the norm for assault education.

The military needs to get serious about making sure its soldiers live up to the creed and that they put teeth back in their regulations which in most cases really just involves enforcing them, especially, when it comes to adultery and integrity. I am dismayed at the acceptance that seems to exist in reference to these issues.

The United States Government is guilty of negligence and purposeful oversight of a very real issue. Change needs to happen. The United States Government is also sue proof for negligence. How many entities can make a law declaring themselves immune from being sued for negligence? The United States Government can, that's who. Just where does accountability lie? Sadly the only recourse for survivors is to speak up. I hope you see the irony in that fact.

The government can spend nine billion dollars redesigning a camouflage pattern and have senate committees for everything including why the neighbor's dog craps in my yard. Just kidding I don't have any neighbors. However I'm sure, knowing the waste that has saturated our government, there is a very real possibility a committee exists for public dog crapping. My daughter, Haley Katherine and all the men and women who are survivors of sexual assault deserve nothing less than answers, an apology and CHANGE.

The fire that burns inside of me that fuels my commitment to my daughter to fight this battle for her and with her is fed in part by my torn feelings of my own service to my country and expectations of those who serve in uniform. For the last 15 years I have worked with the military, primarily but not exclusive with the National Guard. Not as a civilian contractor but as a civilian supporter and volunteer. Being employed in education, high school to be exact, I have come to know many men in uniform who are of high integrity and morals; men who served with professionalism and competence, who were role models to my children as they grew up.

I was privileged enough to spend a week at camp Pendleton in 2000 as part of the Marine Corps outreach and I loved it. I facilitated connecting Katy's third grade class with a soldier who was deployed in Iraq and then went on to write a book about the experience. When our son Zac deployed I facilitated connecting him with a 2nd grade class in our hometown. I was always involved and supportive. When Zac enlisted both his dad and I volunteered at the local armory and became supporters and members of what is called the FRG, Family Readiness Group.

December of 2013 I assumed co lead of the Family Readiness Group we volunteered for and was recently recognized along with other volunteers at an award ceremony. Even though all this was going on with Katy I still helped out and did double duty by staying in touch with her battalions FRG and helping with their Facebook page. I was fortunate enough to garner enough local support to have not only baby blankets made but neat scarves made as well for all the expected and new mothers in the battalion. That meant over 40 baby blankets. I don't tell you this for any other reason than to gain your understanding about how torn I am about the future of my own service, as if there is enough of me left to be torn yet again. It has been so very rough I am profoundly disappointed and heartbroken that I may have to leave all this behind and move on. I'm afraid that I won't be able to deal with my utter disdain for the military and its overall ineptness. It's not the soldiers I can't stand. It's not their fault they all work within the confines of the same web of papers and process that I have had to work through.

The shine and luster of service to my country in the only way I could offer is gone now. And I don't know if I will ever get it back. I believed in the military. I believed in nothing is more a nobler thing to do than to serve your country. But when your country allows shitbags to serve and then makes it so hard for a survivor to obtain any help in any way; it's just wrong. I don't support incompetence; well I guess I do because I pay taxes, which now thinking about it makes me even madder.

It's a messy quagmire of process, paperwork and people that have now consumed my life. Attention from my own private battles is now almost solely focused on Katy's sexual assault. The exchange is not a desirable one. I only wished now that all I had to whine about was my own private issues. A part of me died when Katy was raped. Now I fight for her life so that she can face life and feel the warmth of the sun and God's grace when she looks up. Even after the extensive investigation and what I can hope is a fair trial followed by a first class hanging, Katy will live with this for the rest of her life. Knowing this first hand makes my heart sink with immense sorrow. Her dad and I raised her to live life. We gave her wings to fly and she soared instead. Full of talent, promise, beauty, intelligence, grace and goodness she had her wings clipped by a carnal animal and then she suffered at the hands of incompetence and negligence.

I don't know how much longer Katy and I will be dealing with all the bureaucracy surrounding her rape. But I do know we will fight as hard as we can for what's right for her. I am committed to exploring all options that will be of a benefit for her and to stand up and defend her rights in the process of dealing with it all. Most importantly she has the full support of her entire family and we will never leave her side.

What a difficult task at hand that beautiful young woman has as she tries to heal and recover from a heinous and horrific experience in addition to jumping through the hoops just to obtain the benefits that are supposed to be there for her but that she still has to fight for. Katy continues to impress me with her strength and fortitude. I know she deals with so much silently but that she knows she has to live her life too. While it may appear to others that she doesn't seem to be all that "damaged" by the incident. Those people only see the armor my daughter has built up on the outside. The hurt is on the inside.

Katy has since transferred from the battalion she once proudly served and now is assigned to our local armory. It has been a Godsend to have had that opportunity and I hope it leads to her ultimate decision to not let anything interfere with her dreams. To know how very hard it is for her to put on her uniform yet to see her wearing it serves as motivation for me to carry on as well. We still have so much ahead of us but there will be an end. I will continue to advocate and work with our dear friend, who is her assigned advocate, along with help maneuver through all the procedures and red tape so Katy can focus on being Katy. I don't know how any victim could deal with all the crap involved on their own, even with an advocate there is still so much to handle.

I think if I am told one more time by those individuals I meet along our journey that they realize I am "passionate" about helping my daughter, I will scream. Passionate? That's what you call it? To me that's patronizing. My daughter was raped! To make matters worse the military then exhibited gross negligence in how the matter was handled. I'm not passionate, I'm pissed! No one messes with Momma Cronk's family! I think one way to sum it all up is how I explained myself in an email I sent a while back to one of the numerous individuals I have had to interact with, I told them my claws would put a grizzlies to shame. I think that makes it very clear as to my abilities and intentions.

Katy has her good days when we enjoy the moments and she at least feels a little bit of that sun in her face. When the cloudy days come, they are dark and worrisome to say the least. There are times I am holding a sobbing beautiful young woman who's lost in life because of this. I remember the little girl whose daddy always sang 'You are my sunshine' to. I remember that mowgli faced little girl when she was thinking of how best to frame her big brothers for some heinous crime they didn't really commit. I remember that driven and accomplished young lady we sent off to boot camp and then to war. I know somewhere in that giving and loving heart resides all of those wonderful things that made our Katy so special. I relish at the glimpse of those things as the days go by. And I pray so awful hard for this nightmare to end for her. That she sees justice served and can move on to be better and stronger in spite of it all. I believe she has what it takes, she is Cronk tough. If I had to describe Specialist Haley Katherine Cronk in one word, hands down without a doubt it would be REMARKABLE.

SIXTY

The respite from lamenting of my own private battles and dealing with those that befell Katy brought some interesting revelations to light. I never ever wanted my children to experience on any level anything remotely close to what I have. But then that's not something I have control over. None of us have control of our life but we do have hope and faith. I have always felt that things happen for a reason. They are lessons that can build strength and resolve yet just as easily be used as excuses for failure. I may have learned positivity from Bert, but I learned tenacity from watching my mother. Wrong or right she was tenacious.

If you threw all the bad things that happened to me in a bag and drew them out, expecting me to comment on each one as they were drawn, I would only be able to say, " Ohh...Yeah that time sucked." They all sucked terribly when they were happening. And all these experiences, except for maybe one, I have gone on later in life and by remembering them I was able to learn, grow, understand and sometimes even help someone I loved. Never in my wildest thoughts did I ever think that being molested as a child would come to serve a better purpose when my own daughter was raped.

I look back on my life and I know why I feel strongly about the things that I do. I know why my whole life has been all about my husband and kids.

I haven't spoke to my mother in so long, I haven't kept track. It's sad to say that my life is better for it. I still wonder how she is sometimes and I pray for her but I can't deny the absence of stress and tension in my life. The feelings I have towards my mother are as contradictory as the woman herself. Growing up we always lived in nice places, we always had nice clothes and food on the table. My mother worked hard and did the best she could. Yet she also sabotaged all of it by never acknowledging that she needed help. Things could have been different but not at the expense of my sanity and I hope the Almighty will forgive me. I'm by no means perfect but that doesn't mean I should stop trying to be better.

It has been extraordinarily difficult to find a place in my mind where I can put the drama concerning my parentage. I am an individual in pieces because of it. My loyalty and adoration for the man I knew as my father is unwavering. That will never change. I can even deal with not being a Hilzer anymore mostly because I have been a Cronk for longer and that much I am sure of. What I have problems with, aside from my mother's unwillingness to help me, is the unknown. The 'what if's' run wild in my brain just thinking about all of it. There are people out there I will never meet who I share a parent with.

Most of all by letting it go I feel like I'm condoning what my mother did. Like I'm letting her off the hook and that despite how strongly I feel that she knows more than what she lets on, that I'm letting her get away with it. Then I see what a miserable life she has had by her own hand. And I don't think she has got away with any nasty thing she has done in her life. Besides in the end we all answer to God. I can't let her last betrayal be the one that destroys me. I have come too far and fought too hard to have this be my undoing. Life is a gift and it deserves to be lived.

Everything was wrong in my private life. Everything was out of order. I had to find a way to move forward. I had a very deep desire to put things back where they belonged, to put them in order where I could maybe move forward. So I boxed up all the precious memories of the Hilzer family since the late 1800's that was in the cedar chest and sent the bulk of it back to Colorado to people who were unquestionably Hilzer. I didn't do this as a poor me thing I did it because that wasn't my family; none of it meant anything to me anymore. Overnight all those people whose life was documented by pictures and journals that I had spent my life browsing through were now strangers. It wasn't hard for me to do. It seemed like the right thing to do and I felt really good about returning them to people that were real relation. It was like I was trying to make up for being an imposter all these years. I kept the cedar chest but it now holds my families memories, scrapbooks, mementos. It sits underneath my bedroom window. I keep two pretty pillows on top of it and our kitty Flap Jack spends his afternoons sunning himself on it. When I go to bed and I see the chest sitting there and I think about how it once had Hilzer memories in it and it now has Cronk memories I am reminded that rather than to be filled with the past I'd prefer to work on the future and it is about my family, my husband, my kids.

I wondered what purpose in my life losing my identity could ever serve. I was scared I would be left to wander the rest of my life. I was scared that my life would never be any better and that I was doomed to a continued barrage of bad things because that was really what was in store for my life. I never stopped praying however, my prayers of recent where more full of anger and questions than thankfulness. With each negative prayer my outlook went deeper and deeper in the sewer.

Often times in the early morning as I drive to work I listen to a number of radio preachers and on one morning the topic was thanking God in our prayers even in hard times. I needed that reminder so badly and I took the advice and committed myself to doing just that. It has a been a long road back and I'm not there yet but I am beginning to understand more about what it is I was missing in my life. I am beginning to see a balance of what I lost compared to what I have gained.

For me never in life have I been hung up on material things. God and family have always been first. The material things are life's little extra pleasures but in the end we leave this planet with what we came with, our soul. So when I talk about the things I have gained those are more about being grateful all over again for what I lost sight of. I think complacency was in abundance in my life before my mother's final betrayal. I was just happy being happy that I lost the drive and initiative that I would need to ever have any of my dreams and goals be realized. I just figured God would make it happen. However, faith follows effort alphabetically and so it stands to reason that one must put effort in their faith to realize the dream they had first. I know beyond a doubt that the reunion I have enjoyed with my big brother would not have happened if it weren't for this ordeal. Overall, it has made me recommit to living my life better. By taking away my "past" my mother has actually given me a future that I am starting to feel excited about.

SIXTY ONE

Growing up I have always loved the funny pages. Ziggy was always cute but the cartoon I read first was "Love is…" Each cartoon had some little saying like "Love is… Sharing your last cookie" things like that. There were hundreds of these cartoons, all very cute. In truth I don't believe anyone of us knows what real love is until it's been tested.

In the basement of the church Scott and I got married in, where we had our reception. There was a bulletin board on the wall that had a picture of a teddy bear with a red heart and the caption was "seek with a pure heart". Those words have stuck with me ever since. Lord knows I am no angel, but I do know that making a lifetime commitment to someone means you understand that it's no longer about you. It becomes about us.

Scott and I have a rather unconventional relationship in that we both enjoy witty humor sometimes at the others expense. However, when the circumstances require it, no one else can circle the wagons quicker than us. Through the years we have come to follow each other's lead and become better people individually because of it. I know Scott lived through hell during his addiction and then overcoming it. He has proven his strength and determination to beat decades of self-abuse. He never once stopped trying to be a better man because it got too hard. That is the caliber of a real man. That is the love of my life, my buddy and soul mate.

Both of us are very spiritual. We don't go to church every Sunday but that doesn't lessen our faith. We may have strayed from the path a time or two but God never left our side. It was the good lord that guided us in the hard times and we are very blessed to have been shown such mercy and witnessed such grace.

When I hear Corinthians 13 recited at weddings and such I have to wonder is everyone truly listening?

Love is patient, love is kind. It does not envy, it does not boast, it is not proud. It does not dishonor others, it is not self-seeking, it is not easily angered, and it keeps no record of wrongs. Love does not delight in evil but rejoices with the truth. It always protects, always trusts, always hopes, always perseveres. Love never fails…

That verse is our love story. Kind of a fucked up fairy tale, yet I can't help feeling blessed. It's been a rough long road but I wouldn't trade my troubles for anyone else's, I'm a better person for them. I have no illusions that there will be no more hardships to bear. However, my faith grows stronger with each one. Even when I'm at my lowest and begin to question, that's when I learn the most.

I've decided that I am not going to grow old. I am still growing up. My body may age but my spirit is still young. I have dreams again. I want to travel, go on safari, take cruises, see as much of this beautiful world that I can. I hope the good lord sees fit to make it so that after all these years Scott can retire from being on the road all the time. Most of all I dream about our family and sharing the best years of our life together.

SIXTY TWO

The Lord is my savior, my husband is my strength, my children are my motivation and The Ferluknat Farm is my sanctuary. Ten miles from town I live on a little more than two acres of heaven. It has the most beautiful panoramic view of the Missouri countryside. During the summers it is not unusual that I go for weeks at a time without leaving. Everything I need, I have on my little hobby farm. While I can handle being in public and working with people, it is a necessary task that I must do so that I can support my favorite thing which is to simply create. Other than volunteering at the local armory I really have no social life outside of family. And if my husband would just come around to my way of thinking there would be signs posted on our property that would say 'Turn back now" or Biohazard... Quarantine!!! Possibly even something more direct like... If you made it this far it's only because I had to reload. I like people and I can deal with them on my own terms but overall I just want to be left alone.

Years of being judged have made me judgmental and I try to be vigilant to reverse that. I can be humorously sarcastic and just as easily hurtfully sarcastic. While I try to be accepting of others I have no patience or tolerance for ignorance. While I am a team player I am not a lemming. I like to think for myself and as they say when you're not the lead dog the view never changes. Personally, I'm all about the view.

Living and working on the pipeline my husband taught me two things. First the six P's, they go like this... Prior Planning Prevents Piss Poor Performance. Second and probably my most favorite one to say just for the shock factor is...Excuses are like assholes everyone has one. It never gets old for me. Everyone makes mistakes, including me so I have eaten my words more than I care to admit.

I am definitely a work in progress. I am constantly in motion. I think it's because if I slow down than all the bad things I don't remember can be conjured up by my idol mind. At any given time I have projects lined up in my shop and my craft & sewing room. I love to create beauty in all forms. Each project is prioritized in my mind. I can't move on to the next one until certain tasks or projects are completed. I have so many things I want to do that often times my mind just won't shut down. If only I was like the Flash, I could whip all those projects out in no time. Instead they build up in my mind and drive me crazy.

Telling my story has been on that project list for over 40 years. As a child I dreamed of telling my story because I longed to be understood by my mother. As a teen I wanted to tell my story because I was hurt and angry. As a young mother I wanted to tell my story because I felt alone. Each time it never felt like the right time. The journals I have kept through the years are full of hurt, pain and anger. Shame about being molested and a great amount of hesitation that people I loved would be hurt by my story held me back. I have guarded my privacy for so long that the walls built as defense now are my prison. If I am to break free I feel compelled to share my story so that it wasn't all for nothing.

I love to listen to Joel Osteen but I have read more books by Max Lucado. When the "train wreck" happened in Colorado both Scott and I read Max's book called *Traveling Light*. It's about the 23rd Psalm and about carrying life's baggage with you and how life can be if you just give your worries and troubles to God. The things I have written about are those that I think have come full circle and that by the experience ultimately served a better purpose later in life. Time will tell if justice is served for my daughter and if the military will owe up for what I feel is their negligence and command failure. I live with the very real possibility I will never meet my biological father and thusly find some connection in this world again. Even though these incidents themselves have brought some revelations and understanding to light from my past the door to their answers is yet to open. None the less, I will continue to place my worries and faith in the Almighty. I will keep living my life sunny side up and I will forever be a Crazy Chica!